Praise for *The 9% Edge*

"Candy is an entrepreneur's entrepreneur! She does a masterful job of breaking down and simplifying complex business topics. If you are an entrepreneur, you need this book."

—Tom Hattan, founder and chairman
of Mountainside Fitness

"I love the way Candy thinks. She shows you how to collapse time in a way the most successful people I know have done: breaking down business to the simplest form of the game to create success. This book should be required reading for every high school student, entrepreneur, or anyone who wants to turn the tables on their current situation."

—Rick Steele, founder and executive chairman
of SelectBlinds and PGA Trustee

"People who build real businesses and wealth do things differently. Not only does Candy understand this from her own experience, but she does a masterful job of giving the reader actionable steps to immediately put them on the path to business success. She has cracked the code, and if you're looking to change your reality, this book is for you."

—Todd Davis, retired founder and CEO of LifeLock, Inc.

"Candy has been a huge help to me and to so many other founders I know. Her knowledge has been invaluable in building an eight-figure business and has changed the way I scale my business and diversify wealth. Her wisdom, this book, and its message belongs in the hands of every student, every entrepreneur, and every person who wants to take control of their future, attain success, and create a massively profitable business."

—Amy Lacey, founder of Cali'flour Foods and international
bestselling author

"Candy Valentino is the real deal! She built massive companies and created practical systems to help entrepreneurs and business owners do the same. I highly recommend *The 9% Edge* to anyone who wants to build more revenue, more profit, and more freedom!"

—Rory Vaden, *New York Times* **bestselling author of** *Take the Stairs*

THE

9%

EDGE

CANDY VALENTINO

THE

9 %

EDGE

THE LIFE-CHANGING SECRETS TO CREATE MORE REVENUE FOR YOUR BUSINESS AND MORE FREEDOM FOR YOURSELF

WILEY

Library of Congress Cataloging-in-Publication Data

Names: Valentino, Candy (Candy D.), author. | John Wiley & Sons, publisher
Title: The 9% edge : the life-changing secrets to create more revenue for
  your business and more freedom for yourself / Candy Valentino.
Other titles: Nine percent edge
Description: Hoboken, New Jersey : Wiley, [2025] | Includes bibliographical
  references and index.
Identifiers: LCCN 2024031457 (print) | LCCN 2024031458 (ebook) | ISBN
  9781394152322 (hardback) | ISBN 9781394152346 (adobe pdf) | ISBN
  9781394152339 (epub)
Subjects: LCSH: New business enterprises—Management. | Small
  business—Management. | Revenue management.
Classification: LCC HD62.5 .V327 2025 (print) | LCC HD62.5 (ebook) | DDC
  658.15/54--dc23/eng/20240806
LC record available at https://lccn.loc.gov/2024031457
LC ebook record available at https://lccn.loc.gov/2024031458

Cover Design: Wiley
Cover Image: © phochi/Getty Images
Author Photo: Courtesy of the Author
SKY10082323_082124

*To the millions of entrepreneurs
who dream big dreams, and take big risks –
May you find your edge and use it to create
an even bigger impact in the world.*

Contents

Introduction

The whole point of starting a business is to build a machine that generates revenue and creates wealth, so you can stop trading time for money.

If you are an entrepreneur, business owner, or founder who has laid the foundation of your business and are now looking to grow, scale, and increase your profits – you've come to the right place.

This is *the* guide to growing your revenue, increasing profitability, and creating a business that you can scale (and even potentially exit).

However, that is much easier to say than it is to do. The fact is that 91% of all businesses fail in the first 10 years. This staggering statistic had me questioning why. Was it the wrong business model, a declining market, just bad timing, or was it the founder?

I started to dive in and search to find all the reasons why businesses fail. This led me to a four-year research project with data from thousands of entrepreneurs and their businesses. I was determined to find out if there was a clear correlation in the research.

Turns out, there is. And the reason 9 out of every 10 businesses close their doors before their 10th anniversary may surprise you.

It isn't because they don't have a great idea, or a great product.

It isn't because they don't have a brilliant, Ivy League–educated founder.

It isn't because they didn't master the latest marketing trend or decode the latest social algorithm.

And it isn't due to lack of connections, lack of network, or lack of followers.

The number-one reason businesses fail is summed up in three words: *lack of profit*.

If we expand just slightly on that, the research uncovered these top three reasons: lack of profit, declining sales revenue, and lack of cash flow or funding – aka not enough money.

With this information, I was curious and posed a second question. If we know why 91% of all businesses *fail* in their first 10 years, can we identify what the 9% who *succeed* do differently?

Can we pinpoint, and more importantly duplicate, the patterns of successful, sustainable businesses – and their founders who build them – in order to stack the odds for success in our favor?

The answer is yes, we can. And that is the crux of this book.

Becoming part of the 9% is going to require taking an honest look at your decisions, behaviors, and habits. It's going to require the understanding that what you know *now* might not be the knowledge that you *need* to get where you want to go because some of the skills and habits that got you *here* won't get you *there*.

Building a successful business will require different talents, strategies, and skills to go from startup to growth, to scale, to optimization, and to exit. The skills you developed that helped you start in business are not the same skills you need to sustain in business.

The sooner entrepreneurs understand and apply this principle, the faster you can achieve whatever it is you are after.

What Is This Book Really About?

This is not a flashy book. It's a foundational book. I won't come at you with just theory and concepts. I'll give you tools, principles, and strategies needed to grow, scale, and even exit.

Because if there's only one thing that's true in business, it's that your ability to increase revenue, and ultimately your profit is – and always will be – a primary function and should be a key focus for founders and entrepreneurs.

Your success hinges on your ability to acquire customers, to generate sales, and to maintain profitability, consistently. Growing your revenue and increasing your profitability is not about working harder; it's about working smarter by identifying and implementing key strategies that have a direct impact on your bottom line.

In this book, we're going to dive into all of the details and intricacies of exactly how to do that.

During my 26 years of experience, I've built, scaled, and sold multiple successful businesses in numerous industries. I have also had the pleasure of working with businesses of all sizes – from those making their first couple hundred thousand in revenue, to those doing $200 million, going after an IPO, and creating a unicorn.

The most fascinating thing is that regardless of where you are in your current growth cycle, the principles of creating a scalable, sustainable, and sellable venture remain virtually the same. There are endless ways to architect your build, but when it comes to growth and scale, everything gets boiled down to a handful of core principles.

No matter where you are in your build, all of us entrepreneurs have one seemingly simple thing in common: we want to increase our revenue, keep more of the money we make, and reclaim our freedom in the process. I say seemingly simple because simple doesn't equal easy. If it was easy, more than 9% of us would succeed at doing so.

So whether you're scaling your company, just starting in business, or really ramping up your growth cycle – understanding *how* to increase your revenue, maintain profitability, and create a business that can sustain through the evident challenges that arise is essential to create your edge.

Starting a business is one thing, but consistently growing your revenue and maintaining profitability will require a completely different set of skills.

Throughout this book, we will explore key areas proven to drive business growth, and fundamental principles like expanding your customer base, enhancing average order value, boosting the frequency of purchases, strategically reducing costs (without compromising on quality or service), and how to measure and evaluate the critical revenue drivers in your business.

This book is not about quick fixes or overnight success. It's about applying consistent, focused efforts to strengthen the core aspects of your business. Whether you are looking to fine-tune your operations or need a complete overhaul on your finances, the insights shared here will give you the edge and secure your place within the 9%, making your success not just possible or probable, but predictable.

We are going to go deep in all the ways you can increase your revenue NOW, what levers you can pull to increase your profit NOW, and ultimately how to buy back your time and create more freedom NOW.

Who Am I to Help?

Well, here's the thing. If you want to learn from someone with an MBA or a PhD, or a dozen other letters after their name, that's not me. I don't have a business degree, I didn't come from a wealthy or educated family, and quite honestly I don't use perfect grammar or sentence structure (drives my editor nuts!). I'm not a writer, I'm not a professional speaker, and I'm not some online marketer. I'm an entrepreneur – just like you.

I've taken risks, I've had huge successes and massive failures, and have figured out a lot over the last two and half decades. What I lack in institutional education, I make up for in real-world application.

I didn't invent a market-disrupting idea, I didn't reengineer an industry, and I didn't perfectly time a vertical roll-up. Instead, I simply had the willingness to try, the commitment to continue, and enough leverage to keep showing up, even when I didn't want to – and the beautiful part is that these are all things you can do, too. All these things are within your ability and your control. Because success, my friend, is far less about what resources you have, and far more about how resourceful you are willing to be.

So whether you read my words, hear me speak, or tune into *The Candy Valentino Show*, you know that I don't teach from books, from theory, or from regurgitated information I heard from someone on the internet. I teach from experience, from exploration, from trying and failing, from being relentless in the pursuit of knowledge and growth. And if I'm really good at any one thing, it's actually just identifying patterns, understanding numbers, and simplifying complex topics. That's it. No earth-shattering inventions or genius IQ here.

Prior to all the businesses, the investments, and the books, I was born in a single-wide, little white trailer parked on the outskirts of a small town. My parents, teenagers when I was born, relied on government assistance to make ends meet. My early years were marked by the hardships of poverty and abuse. With no option for childcare, I spent my afternoons and evenings in my father's small auto repair shop, witnessing the struggles of entrepreneurship firsthand.

Most of the kids I knew had after-school routines of learning the mechanics of some sport, dance, or gymnastics. I, on the other hand, was learning the mechanics of small business – inside the walls of a greasy, grimy little garage. My mom cleaned houses, my dad turned wrenches (as he called it), and I witnessed the immense amount of hard work it takes to put food on the table.

I worked with my dad every day until I turned 16. Immediately after high school, recognizing that the traditional route of college would not fast-track me to where I needed to be, I secured an SBA loan with a six-week run-rate and launched my first brick-and-mortar venture.

My journey didn't stop with that first successful enterprise. I expanded into product manufacturing, launched additional businesses, created additional locations, scaled service and consulting businesses, launched an SaaS company, acquired and consolidated businesses, successfully exited three companies, and built a significant real estate portfolio in the process.

The important thing is this: I didn't have connections, resources, money, or a corporate background filled with talents and skills. But that's the best part – because success is truly here for all of us. Regardless of your childhood, your background, your level of education, or your reality right now, with an intentional plan, determination, and commitment to continue, and the knowledge and understanding to architect your build – truly anything is possible.

For me, those efforts allowed me to create a nonprofit and donate a building to the organization in my early 20s, marking the beginning of my long-standing commitment to philanthropy, which I've continued over the last 20 years. Financial success can be a catalyst to create real impact in the world.

Who Is This Book For?

The strategies and insights I share in this book are not theoretical musings, but lessons from the real business world as experience from doing has been my greatest teacher. In business, we only learn one of two ways: from mentors or from our mistakes. My hope is to save you from the latter by sharing this knowledge and research with you.

I've helped multiple businesses turn around from the brink of failure to revamp their financial structure and create a path toward profit. I've consulted with others who were stable, successful, and ready to scale to their next revenue benchmark. Each case was unique, yet the underlying principles remained consistent and the outcomes have been transformative.

Along with my research, these experiences have not only solidified my approach to business, but also deepened my commitment to empowering others. The essence of this book is not just to share knowledge, but to offer you actual tools and strategies that can elevate your business to a new level of growth and success – all aimed at helping you increase profit, achieving more freedom, and finding your edge to become part of the 9%.

As we get into the core strategies and practices to business growth, remember this: the principles I share are universal and proven. So whether you're aiming for your first $100,000, navigating your first couple million, or pushing past $30 million in revenue – this book is for you.

By the time you finish reading this book, you'll have a new level of clarity, a greater understanding of your financial picture, and the practical steps to take next. All of this will make building a business easier, faster, and more profitable than ever before.

So get ready – you're on the verge of more revenue, more profit, and more freedom, NOW.

Let's get started.

PART I

More Revenue NOW

CHAPTER 1

Architecting an Intentional Business

If you are not intentionally building a business, you will accidentally build yourself a job.

N o matter how good you are, and no matter how long you've been at this, the reality is that 91% of all businesses fail within 10 years.

According to the US Small Business Administration (SBA), around 66% of all new businesses make it to the two-year mark, only half of all companies survive past five years, and more than 90% fail within 10 years.

And it's not just small businesses that suffer this fate. I almost fell off my chair when I learned that 88% of all the Fortune 500 companies that existed just 50 years ago are gone. They have either gone completely bankrupt, crashed, or been eaten up in a merger, and even those few that still exist are no longer a Fortune 500 company.[1]

Steven Denning, a Forbes senior contributor, pointed out that 50 years ago the life expectancy of a Forbes 500 company was 75 years.[2] Today, it's less than 15 years![3] This means you will likely outlive some of the biggest companies that exist today.

That was a lot of data, but stay with me. This is all-important for you and your business.

In his study of hundreds of startups, Harvard Business School professor Tim Eisenmann found that while business owners may have the right acumen and decision-making skills, a whole host of issues can lead to the demise of a small business. One of these issues is the philosophy of "just start" – a message I see shared over and over again on social media. And while there is truth to starting before you *feel* ready, there is also truth in not starting before you're actually ready.

Hear me out. You'll never feel fully ready to do anything. There will always be a feeling of needing "one more." One more year to prepare, one more degree on the wall, one more person more capable than you, one more pass at the manuscript to make it better – oh wait, that one was me. ;)

Entrepreneurs who blindly follow the advice of "just start" will often skip crucial elements needed to build a successful business. They miss establishing key components like market research, investigating customer demand, ideal customer demographics, and job markets for hiring employees, to name a few.

I find that startup entrepreneurs are so eager to get started that they set themselves up to fail (or fizzle out) before they even launch.

Being strategic and having intention about what you're building is more important than starting at all. Without proper planning, you could wake up one day realizing you built a business you hate, or a job you have to show up for.

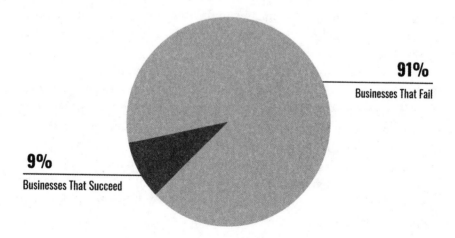

91%
Businesses That Fail

9%
Businesses That Succeed

Building with Intention

Every business is unique, even within the same industry, same vertical, same market, or even the same town. The business is as unique as the founder's fingerprint, making the path to success unpredictable. But when you combine a few key principles – which we will break down throughout this book – you can start to change the odds in your favor. The first principle is always building a business with intention.

When your business has a clear purpose, and you are deeply intentional in your build, you will have better beliefs, which will create better decisions, which will create better behaviors, which will create better habits, and in turn that will create better results.

Starting with a clearly defined purpose and deeply intentional plan is like the difference between being busy and being productive. You can be really busy and achieve nothing that matters. You can be really excited and achieve nothing that matters, or at least doesn't propel you closer to your ultimate goal. You can work endless hours, and still fail. You can join all the groups, learn all the latest marketing hacks, create an audience, customers, products, and funnels, and still fail.

Why? **Because not all action is created equal.** Setting goals and achieving them creates momentum. But not all momentum is valuable. Undirected momentum is reckless. Setting intentional goals and directing momentum – now that is rocket fuel.

in·ten·tion·al·i·ty[4]

/in¸ten(t)SHə'nalədē/

noun

the fact of being deliberate or purposive.

the quality of mental states (e.g., thoughts, beliefs, desires, hopes) that consists in their being directed toward one object or state of affairs.

A study from the *Journal of Small Business and Enterprise Development*[5] observed entrepreneurs as they developed their businesses to evaluate and better understand what they consider motivating factors in their decision-making. Over 600 entrepreneurs participated in the study. I analyzed the findings of this study and four others completed in prior years. I added my own research from evaluating, working with, and researching entrepreneurs and included the data points here.

I found that there are four main **Entrepreneurial Triggers** (what causes someone to become an entrepreneur). One, however, was exponentially larger than the other three.

Three of the four main Entrepreneurial Triggers are:

1. **Existing negative conditions:** I don't like my job, don't like my boss, don't like my co-workers, or the job was boring (18%).
2. **Future potential outcomes:** I had an idea, I saw a problem to solve, I saw a market/need for this business (12%).
3. **Current circumstantial challenge:** I inherited a business, joined my family's business, or a loved one passed away (8%).

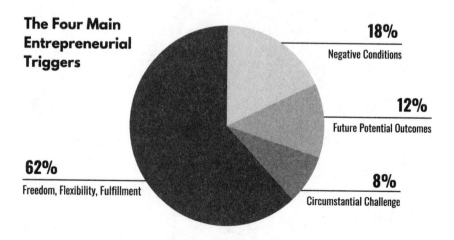

The Four Main Entrepreneurial Triggers

18%
Negative Conditions

12%
Future Potential Outcomes

62%
Freedom, Flexibility, Fulfillment

8%
Circumstantial Challenge

But almost two-thirds of the entrepreneurs studied (62%) fell into the fourth and largest section of Entrepreneurial Triggers. This Entrepreneurial Trigger is based on the need for personal freedom, control of schedule, desiring more fulfillment, realizing true potential, achieving a dream, and a yearning for personal and professional growth.

I call it the **Freedom, Flexibility, and Fulfillment Triad.**

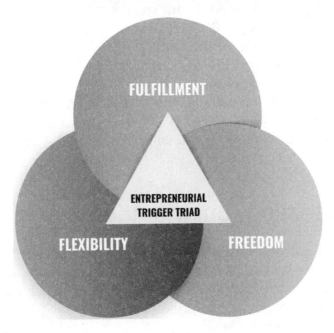

So when reading through all the research that the team and I uncovered, I posed this question: If we can find the commonality in why businesses are started, can we also show why (and more importantly, how) businesses succeed? The answer is yes.

Since 91% of all businesses fail and only 9% succeed, what does the 9% do differently? One factor between 9% and the 91% is the presence, or absence, of **intentional behavior**.

Entrepreneurs who chose to actively further their knowledge, increase their skills, and be intentional with their behavior guided themselves to make choices with the end in mind rather than making decisions based on where they are right now. Those decisions based on future projection radically shifted their current (and future) behavior, which created drastically different habits, which in turn gave them extraordinary results.

On the contrary, the entrepreneurs who chose not to increase their knowledge, increase their skills, and be international with their decisions exhibited erratic behavior, keeping the entrepreneur stuck in busy work, operating more like a hamster on the perpetual entrepreneurial wheel than a builder who carefully and strategically architects their master plan.

Either way, you choose. And if you don't choose, remember you still choose. Choices you don't make are still choices – they are just choices that are made for you. Because if you choose not to act on building a business with intention, circumstances beyond your control will force you to act anyway.

Remember, businesses run on a system that has internal logic, form, and function, and follows its own momentum. Whether a business will grow or whether it will eventually fail is at first determined by the intentionality, or lack thereof, of its founder.

Architecting Your Intention

Without a clear strategy and intentional plan, it's easy to find yourself trapped in a business that demands your constant attention, time, and focus. Many entrepreneurs fall into the trap of effectively creating a self-employed job, and not a scalable business.

So how can we avoid this?

In my book *Wealth Habits* I cover the importance of starting with the end in mind, regardless of what goal you're after. I call it REO (which always makes me think of REO Speedwagon, but I digress) – Reverse Engineered Outcomes.

Unlike the common and conventional ways of dealing with problems, REO starts with the end in mind and how what we believe, how we think, act, decide, and behave is in alignment with the desired end result.

By focusing on the desired outcome and reverse engineering the target, we are able to better create the results we want with efficiency and with greater speed.

The most successful companies, athletes, inventors, and Olympians all leverage reverse engineering to achieve significant results.

Leveraging pattern recognition, creativity, strategic thinking, and skill arbitrage helps us look beyond the surface and find the hidden structure. In doing so, you can achieve just about anything, and do so with greater speed and efficiency.

Let's look at the eight steps to Reverse Engineer Outcomes.

The Eight Steps to Reverse Engineer Outcomes

1 **Identify the Problem:** What is the current challenge, constraint or problem that you are trying to solve?

_____

_____

_____

2 **Define Your Target:** Clearly define the desired outcome.
What is your desired goal?

_____

_____

_____

3 **Narrow Your Focus:** Find solutions that will help you achieve the desired result.
What are three specific things you need to do to help you achieve the desired result?

_____

_____

_____

4 **Frame Your View:** Look for current strengths and opportunities by framing the right questions to help you achieve this. What questions can you ask yourself to help find alternate solutions?

_____

_____

_____

5 **Refine Your Plan:** What support do you need, what data or metrics need to be analyzed, who could help with this, what else is needed, what is possible?

_____

_____

_____

6 **Choose Your Solution:** Identify any and all possible solutions that could help achieve this.

_____

_____

_____

7 **Design Your Plan:** What would need to happen in order for you to solve this goal in 90 days or less?

_____

_____

_____

8 **Take Action:** What are the next best steps you need to implement within the next 48 hours to achieve this?

_____

_____

_____

These eight steps make the REO method an extremely productive and practical way of progressing toward your desired outcome, giving you the ability to condense time and move forward with speed.

One example of a successful REO was Southwest Airlines. The company was experiencing an expensive problem with their planes. It took them approximately 40 minutes to refuel each airplane. With more than 700 aircraft operating over 4,000 flights per day, this inefficiency created a very costly problem.

When first addressing this problem, the Southwest leadership teams asked, "Why are these planes spending so much time on the ground?" They went on to discuss all the reasons why the planes took so much time to refuel. Because of the way they posed the question, they were unable to find a solution.

When they changed their approach and framed it in a way that aligned with their desired outcome, they asked one simple straightforward question: "How can we get the planes to spend less time on the ground?"

The ideas began to flow like jet fuel. This change in approach led Southwest to adopt a new solution that took refueling from 40 minutes to 12 minutes. This shift drastically reduced expenses while increasing profitability and efficiency, as well as operational performance and customer satisfaction.

Another company that displayed immense intention to reverse engineer their desired outcome was Tesla. Elon Musk reverse engineered the technology used by companies that created the batteries for laptops. This approach allowed him to see how a similar design could potentially work in electric vehicles and gave the company massive insight to create a product that was more efficient. Asking the right questions and being intentional with architecting a plan put them on a path of innovation and success that's been unparalleled in the automotive industry. Taking time to craft their model and refine their path in the beginning avoided the endless challenges and delays in getting to market and made their path to success seem like it happened overnight.

Reverse engineering can both decrease your costs and increase your efficiency drastically. The time, discipline, and intentionality of launching took years. Had Tesla followed the common phrase on social media "just start!" they would likely have been "dead on arrival."

When you are looking to reverse engineer a goal, an outcome like Southwest did, or even a product like Tesla did, here are some thought-provoking questions to ponder:

- What patterns can you identify from established businesses and leading companies within your industry?
- What techniques do industry leaders use to increase revenue, attract high-level talent, streamline processes, or have better functionality?

- How can you effectively apply the knowledge you found or have gained to improve your business, your revenue, or your products?

Your Business Shelf Life

Every business has a shelf life. From the day you open the doors to the last day you close them, every business starts and eventually ends. Even if you build a scalable, sustainable, and sellable business, and become part of the most viable and long-lasting businesses in the country – with the likes of JP Morgan, Colgate, Jim Beam, and Cigna – your time within that business will still end.

Whether it fails and closes its doors for good, whether you pass it on to your children or your family, or whether you sell it, merge, or are acquired – the harsh reality is this: every founder will exit their business at some point. Whether you get paid for it or not is up to you, and ultimately the intentionality you have with its build. Architecting with intention can be a significant factor that determines not only your ability to have a capital exit, but how much you get paid for it in the process.

The hard truth is that more than 75%–80% of businesses will never be acquired, meaning you have an almost 8 out of 10 chance that your business will *not* be an asset and that you need to invest wisely so that one day you can retire – or at least make work optional since most of us don't ever really want to retire.

If your goal is to build a company that is an asset, one that you can eventually cash out at the exit, how different would your decisions be now with that plan in mind?

Imagine how you'd handle situations and choices if you framed each decision through the lens of an eventual exit or acquisition. How would you answer that question, how would you make that decision, who would your next hire be, and how important is understanding business finance? How would you show up differently in your business if you had the intention of building a business you could exit?

For the first 15 years of my journey running multiple businesses – leading teams, more locations, industries, and real estate investing projects – I kept myself on the entrepreneurial hamster wheel. Because even though I had people, profits, and processes in place, I still didn't think I could leave my businesses. So I never went on a week's vacation. I'd take long weekends, but never full weeks. The thought of leaving would give me anxiety because I knew the overwhelming workload that would await my return. Returning to the office after four days was a nightmare and I couldn't imagine the chaos a week off would create. Initially, I didn't realize that I essentially built a cage for myself, the exact opposite of the freedom and flexibility I desired.

I knew I could go on a vacation, but looking back I simply didn't want to. Buried in work, wearing the badge of busy, can be a great place to hide. My conscious decision fueled by some unconscious wiring kept me on that hamster wheel so long that 15 years in, I found myself burned out, stressed out, and utterly exhausted. I ran so hard and so long that I ran myself straight into the ground.

Many entrepreneurs I work with get caught in this trap, too. Instead of following the trigger that made them want to be an entrepreneur to begin with – the freedom and flexibility to spend time with family, to control their own schedule, to be able to casually visit their favorite coffee shop on a Tuesday – they got caught up working almost entirely in or on the business, and they found themselves not having the time to do what they originally envisioned, or feeling guilty when they did.

So I want to ensure you're extremely intentional about *what* you want to build so that you can avoid the number-one mistake entrepreneurs make – where you think you're creating a business, but you inadvertently create a job. Unless you're planning to work forever, you need to establish a system that generates income, brings in consistent revenue, and builds wealth – so you can have what everyone ultimately wants: freedom.

So now that I laid the foundation of *why* it's important to do this, let's discuss *how* to do this.

Having built multiple companies and businesses, and working with thousands of entrepreneurs, I've identified a consistent through line pattern with what it takes to construct a scalable, sustainable, and sellable model regardless of the industry or vertical you're in.

Building that model starts with architecting an intentional business, and reverse engineering the vision and goal you have for your business altogether. But to become part of the elusive 9%, it doesn't stop there.

There is a roadmap to your business success, but before we jump into the rest of that process, there are some common landmines you'll need to avoid along the way.

Let's break those down now so while you're navigating and architecting your build, you can avoid the most common traps that can trip you up and prevent you from getting there.

CHAPTER 2

Common Entrepreneurial Landmines to Avoid

Your greatest expansion will come from refinement and elimination.

"I'm sorry, honey, I can't make it."

Tears streamed down little Kailey's cheeks as she heard those words on the other end of the phone. "But Daddy, you missed the last one, too."

His heart sank and his eyes became instantly wet as he slowly swallowed the guilt down the back of his throat. "I know, honey, but Daddy can't leave work right now. I'll be at the next one, I promise." They both let out a sigh as if they quietly acknowledged an empty promise that wouldn't be fulfilled.

"Okay, Daddy," she said as her voice cracked. They ended the call and John went back to the papers on his desk. As he reflected on that call and their exchange with yet another broken promise, he thought back to why he started this business in the first place.

It was winter, three years ago. Kailey was just in preschool. John stood gazing out of his office window. The cold pane of glass separated him from the outside, but it couldn't separate him from the disappointment he felt. "DENIED" the request form was marked, this time for vacation between Christmas and New Year's. "Someone more senior already requested these dates. Sorry, John, maybe next year," the rep from HR said.

The pit in his stomach grew larger, and anger started to creep in. For years, John had poured his heart and soul into his job, hoping for that promotion, only to be overlooked time and again. But today, the rejection stung a little deeper than ever before.

As he watched the snow consume the city streets below, that anger manifested into an idea. He made the decision, right then and there, that he wasn't waiting for permissions and promotions anymore – that to have the life he wanted for himself and his family, he had to go out on his own.

He took every dime they had in savings, rented a small office on the corner of town, and decided to go "all in" on himself.

Years passed, and John's business flourished.

During one quiet evening, as the snow fell yet again outside his office window, he received that FaceTime call from Kailey. With the dim glow of his office lamp reflecting on the cold pane of glass, John could see the disappointment in his daughter's face. He realized with a pang of regret that while he had been building this company, he had inadvertently distanced himself from the very reason he had embarked on this journey – to provide a better life for his family, to be present, front row and center in their lives.

He felt disappointment yet again, only this time wasn't because someone else let him down; it was because he let his family down again.

Looking at the snow consuming the streets once again, he realized he had gotten trapped in the **Entrepreneurial Landmines of a Business**. While trying to build a business filled with flexibility and freedom, he inadvertently created a cage for himself. But this time, he held the key to his freedom in his own pocket. It was going to take an intentional decision – to redesign and rebuild his business – to open the lock.

He started understanding his numbers, started delegating responsibilities, empowering his team, hiring more people, and one by one began eliminating his roles in the business, all of which enabled him to carve out time for what mattered most – moments like showing up for Kailey.

Despite the reward of building a successful business, John found himself in one of the common traps entrepreneurs make – a trap where entrepreneurship morphs from a golden opportunity to golden handcuffs.

As we acknowledge the common pitfalls that will trip up, entrap, or enslave entrepreneurs, I caution you that they can often be disguised as markers of success. The sobering truth is that John's story is more than a cautionary tale – it's demonstrating the bridge between aspiration and reality, between ideation and execution.

Let's cover the six most common traps entrepreneurs face.

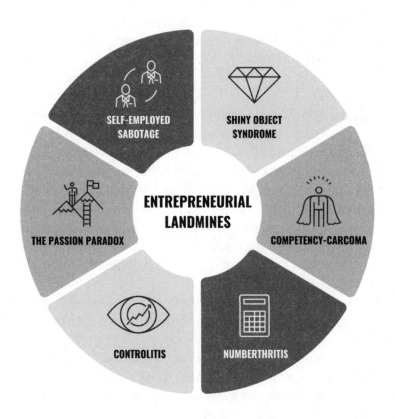

Entrepreneur Landmine #1: Self-Employed Sabotage

Self-Employed Sabotage, also known as the plight of the solopreneur, is characterized by a high degree of personal involvement. As the business owner, you're integral to its operations, from client interactions to product creation. While this offers direct control over quality and customer experience, it also can limit your freedom and scalability. The business's success is inseparably linked to *your* continuous effort, making it challenging to take time off or to step away without impacting the business's performance, and your bottom line.

Self-Employed Sabotage consumes many hopeful startup founders. If you're not careful, you'll find yourself not creating a business at all. Instead you'll wake up one day like John – whether it's one year, five years, or 10 years down the road – realizing you've spent all of this time creating a job you need to show up for every day.

With proper planning and intention, you can avoid this landmine. It requires building a company that not only generates revenue in your absence but also one that becomes an asset and offers the potential for an eventual exit.

Understanding the intention of the business, and properly delegating, eliminating, and automating its functions, is paramount in avoiding this landmine. But keep in mind, no business model is free of challenge. Building a scalable, sustainable. and sellable model also offers its own difficulties. Yes, it's designed to operate independently of the owner's day-to-day involvement, emphasizing systems, processes, teams, and strategic planning. And yes, this approach can increase personal freedom, and also enhances the business's value – because its success is not solely reliant on any single individual – but it also can present challenges.

Depending on which role you serve in your business, and which role you enjoy, the scalable model can pose its own difficulties, which we will cover in depth in Chapter 3.

This enigma is why there isn't a "one size fits all" business. Instead it's about building a "one size that fits YOU" business. Aligning your business with your personal goals, and the life you want to create, now *and* in the future – that is the utmost goal.

Before we progress, let's assess how you're currently operating in your business.

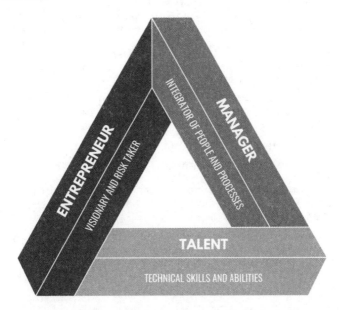

Entrepreneur, Manager, Talent: Which Role Are YOU?

1 When thinking about starting a project or business, which of these statements resonates with you the most?

   a. I am most excited about creating or perfecting the product/service itself.
   b. I enjoy organizing how the project/business will operate and leading the team towards our goals.
   c. I am energized by the challenge and potential rewards of taking financial and strategic risks.

2 Where do you derive your energy in a work setting?

   a. From using my skills and creativity to create or improve something tangible.
   b. From managing people, improving processes, and achieving operational efficiency.
   c. From identifying opportunities, navigating uncertainties, and achieving growth.

3 In a group project or business venture, what role do you naturally gravitate towards?

   a. The one who generates ideas and brings them to life with my technical skills or creative talent.
   b. The one who plans, delegates, and ensures the project is on track to meet its objectives.
   c. The one who looks at the bigger picture, makes key financial decisions, and drives the project towards greater achievement.

4 When faced with a critical decision, which approach do you typically take?

   a. I base my decisions on how they will affect the quality and integrity of the work or product.
   b. I consider what is most efficient and effective for the team and the project's success.
   c. I weigh the potential risks and rewards, looking for the decision that offers the best opportunity to achieve our desired outcome.

5 How do you react when faced with significant setbacks or challenges?

  a. I focus on refining my service or product to overcome the challenge.
  b. I reorganize resources, focus on the team and adjust strategies to navigate through the situation.
  c. I see it as an opportunity to learn, adapt, and make bold moves that could lead to even greater success on the other side.

6 When considering improvements in work or business, which of these focuses most appeal to you?

  a. Innovating something new or improving the quality of my product/service.
  b. Optimizing existing processes, making the team more effective, and improving delivery.
  c. Expanding the market, exploring new business opportunities, or scaling operations.

7 How do you prefer to receive feedback on your work or project?

  a. I value feedback that helps me improve the creativity and technical aspects of my work.
  b. I value feedback that focuses on how well the team is functioning and meeting goals.
  c. I value feedback that evaluates the leadership, or the potential growth and opportunity of the business.

8 Which of these learning opportunities excites you the most?

  a. Trainings, seminars or workshops that enhance my craft, skill, or artistic ability.
  b. Leadership training, courses on management practices, or systems optimization.
  c. Seminars on leadership, market trends, investment, and risk management.

9 Who do you admire most?

  a. Highly skilled individuals who have made significant contributions to their field.
  b. Effective leaders or managers who have built cohesive and high-performing teams.
  c. Successful founders who have taken bold risks and built influential businesses.

10 When you think about your future, which of these scenarios sounds most appealing?

  a. Being recognized as a leading expert or innovator in my field, known for my unique contributions.
  b. Leading a team or organization to become the best in its class, known for operational excellence.
  c. Building or investing in businesses that redefine industries and generate significant revenue or impact.

Mostly A's: Your strengths align most with the Talent role.
You have a profound connection to the craft and artistry of your work, whether it's through innovation, creativity, or specialized skill. Your passion lies in the act of creation itself, working with customers, or bringing new ideas or products to life. You are being driven by passion and the love of what you do. Your strengths are creativity, developing skills with excellence and a unique personal touch on your business.

Mostly B's: Your strengths align most with the Manager role.
You are built for organizing, directing, and optimizing. You thrive on making systems and organizations more efficient, building and leading high-performing teams, and ensuring that the operational side of a project or the short-term needs of the business, runs smoothly and efficiently. Your strengths are leadership, strategic thinking, and problem-solving.

Mostly C's: Your strengths align most with the Entrepreneur role.
You are driven by the challenge and thrill of building something from the ground up. Your focus is on identifying opportunities, taking calculated risks, and driving growth and innovation in the business landscape. You inject energy and innovation into businesses or industries, pushing the boundaries of what's possible. Your strengths are visionary thinking, resilience, and risk management.

Entrepreneur Landmine #2: The Passion Paradox

I just took a long deep breath as I write this, because I know I'm going to get a lot of hate for this one. But this philosophy trips up many people, so here we go anyway.

Many of these "online gurus" you follow will tell you to "follow your passion" and create a business. But let me guess – they are trying to sell you a course or a program, or be your coach on how to create a business to follow your passion.

It's such garbage advice.

And look, you don't have to take my word on it; numerous studies have proven it. According to the findings of three Stanford researchers, this advice can be detrimental to your success. Trying to find a passion to follow can create narrowmindedness and dedication to a single, isolated interest and cause you to miss numerous other important factors.[1]

Another study, led by Erica Bailey at Columbia Business School, found that those who were self-described "passionate" were also more likely to be overconfident. That overconfidence can lead to detrimental work outcomes, because they are less likely to seek the feedback and information necessary. She found that being too passionate about your work may lead to an inflated view of your own abilities and work output.[2]

Instead of building a business around a passion, how about we build a business that generates positive cash flow so you can have time and freedom – to follow any passion you want.

And no, I am not suggesting you build a business you hate. We don't have to live in such extremes. It's simply that the philosophy of "love what you do every day" is an old, overused cliché that's been regurgitated across social media feeds, self-help books, seminar stages, and even touted by "coaches" with no research or context. And, quite frankly, it is harmful and can be detrimental.

Here's the science on the challenges of what I call the Passion Paradox:

1. **The statement implies we have one passion.**
    I don't know anyone who is passionate about one singular thing. Ask any parent what they are passionate about and they'll

say their kids; ask any dog lover what they are passionate about and they'll say their dog – that doesn't mean you want to start a business around kids or dogs. People have more than one interest, and selecting just one passion narrows your focus and prevents other ideas from being uncovered.

2. **The statement implies our passions don't change with time.**

   We continually evolve in every stage of our lives. What you are passionate about and love to do in your 20s will likely not be the same in your 40s. We are constantly changing, and that means our passions will likely change, too.

3. **The statement implies we know what our passion is.**

   Many people have no clue what their passion is, let alone how they can tie it to a business. If this is you, you're not alone. You need time, exploration, and exposure to many different things in life before you're able to even know what you're passionate about. Trying to tie your life's work to your passion is an instant source of stress and anxiety. And then you think something is wrong with you because you haven't found "your passion" yet. (FYI, there isn't anything wrong with you.)

4. **The statement implies that your passion can be monetized in a way that aligns with your goals.**

   Just because you have a passion for something doesn't mean you're good at it, nor does it mean you can monetize it. I may be passionate about singing, but it doesn't mean I'm any good at it. So imagine I build a business or career around singing, but no one hires me because I suck. If you aren't good at your chosen passion, you're unlikely to make money at it, which will ultimately be frustrating and defeating.

5. **The statement implies shifting your passion to a business won't change the way you feel about it.**

   This is the bright-red flashing sign most people miss. If you turn doing something you love into something for monetary gain, your passion may very well lose the feeling it once had. No matter what business or job you have, there are going to be days when you are not passionate about working with that client, handling that employee, or running that webinar. Starting a business around a passion is only going to get you so far no matter how much you love it. If you have to show up all the time, handle all the challenges, and deal with all the employees, it too becomes work.

A passion can be a hobby instead of a profession. It can be something that lights you up, or provides you with great joy – and that doesn't need to be monetized.

The goal should be to build a business and a life that aligns with who you are and what you can be successful at. If you *mostly* enjoy what you do, you will be able to outrun, outlast, and out-survive anyone in your industry.

Your "passion" for building a business could be freedom, it could be time, it could be to attend every one of your kids' baseball games, it could be to work from home, it could be to travel with your spouse; it could also be to ring the opening bell, to disrupt an industry, to reimagine a product, to solve a problem for people, to create generational wealth, or to give and donate as much as you want.

Building an organization that gives you what you truly want – that's the name of the game. Once you achieve that, you'll likely find yourself in the elusive 9% with not only a successful business, but also a *rich life*.

Obviously, I unsubscribed from the philosophy of building businesses around your passion. What's far more important is to build a model that aligns with your current and future goals, as well as one that is congruent with who you are. But you can decide for yourself. The unsubscribe button is always there for you.

Entrepreneur Landmine #3: Shiny Object Syndrome

There can be great challenge with being so singularly focused on a "passion," and there can also be great challenge on the complete opposite of the spectrum: being so distracted that you have little to no focus.

The demands on the entrepreneur are great, you're wearing multiple hats, juggling dozens of balls in the air at once, often feeling like the weight of the world is on your shoulders (which is actually the weight of risk and responsibility). Then pair this with modern technologies that put additional demands on our attention and our focus. The distractions put in our path have never been greater, and if we're not careful, we'll lose both.

When we look back to even just the 1980s – prior to the rise of personal communications and computing devices – the bid for our attention has increased 500%. These distractions also impact our productivity and in turn decrease our efficiency and overall results.

The cure for **Shiny Object Syndrome** is the **Expansion Equation:**

$$Goals + Focus - Distraction = Expansion$$

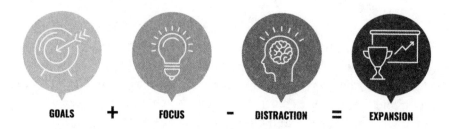

GOALS **+** FOCUS **−** DISTRACTION **=** EXPANSION

When applied consistently, with discipline, not only will you achieve your goals, but you will condense time and operate with speed. This makes your attention and your focus two of your most valuable business commodities.

Although we often think the path toward our goals is through *adding* more things, more commonly, the opposite is true.

Expansion comes from elimination.

It seems like a contradiction, doesn't it? Expansion through elimination?

After analyzing the largest corporations and companies in the world, researching and interviewing some of the most successful founders in the world, plus personally working with hundreds of companies, not to mention my own, I realized the most successful entrepreneurs all have an ability to refine and eliminate.

From tech giants to retail behemoths, the common thread is clear: a relentless focus on core competencies and a ruthless willingness to eliminate anything that doesn't contribute to the bottom line. They all know how to streamline their offerings, and their operations, for maximum profitability.

One of my very first consulting clients, Emily, is a great example of this. She owned a marketing firm that offered everything from email marketing and building websites to social media management, influencer marketing, running affiliate programs, PR campaigns, ad management, event promotions – yet she wasn't able to break past the $3 million benchmark in revenue.

I evaluated her business and we discussed what efforts were crippling her profitability. She got caught up trying to do "all of the things," which was draining her focus, her time, and ultimately her bottom line. I asked Emily if she was ready to build her business in a completely different way, which would require her to make a bold decision. She said was up for the challenge.

We began to systematically trim the excess that had weighed down her firm. We evaluated and analyzed which offerings, clients, and areas of operations could be scaled back. She let go of clients that weren't as profitable, and refocused resources on the core business of PR and events. She also reduced the number of service offerings they promoted, allowing Emily to redirect her energy toward understanding the needs of her target customer, enhancing the quality of the services she offered, training the team to provide better customer experience, and creating more success for the clients she served.

In just nine months of this reorganization, she increased her top-line revenue by 58% and profitability by 61%, breaking far past the evasive $3 million benchmark she'd been trying to hit for three years.

This speaks to a valuable lesson: true growth often requires the courage to let go. In a world obsessed with the constant and relentless pursuit of more, sometimes the path to success lies not in accumulation, but in refinement.

Evaluating whether you are succumbing to profit-destroying distractions requires a combination of self-awareness, analysis, and even feedback. So it all comes down to being in control of your focus.

Focus is an invaluable commodity.

Here are a few ways to evaluate what could be destroying focus (and ultimately your bottom line).

Self-Reflection

Regularly take time to reflect on your business practices, priorities, and goals. Ask yourself questions such as:

- Am I spending my time and resources on activities that align with my long-term objectives?
- Do I find myself frequently shifting focus or chasing after new opportunities without fully evaluating their impact?
- Am I effectively delegating tasks and empowering my team, or am I overly involved in day-to-day operations?

Review Objectives

Revisit your objectives and key performance indicators (KPIs) to help assess whether your actions are contributing to the overall success of the business. And evaluate if your current activities are aligned with these objectives or if they are being diverted by distractions.

Get Feedback

Employees, peers, and mentors can provide valuable perspective. Employees may be able to offer insights into workflow inefficiencies or areas where micromanagement is impeding productivity.

SWOT

Finally, this is my personal favorite and go-to: conduct a SWOT (Strengths, Weaknesses, Opportunities, Threats) analysis. This can help identify areas of vulnerability or distraction within your business or even your day.

Evaluating strengths and weaknesses alongside opportunities and threats will help you prioritize actions to capitalize on strengths and mitigate weaknesses that may be contributing to distractions.

Being pulled in too many directions can negatively impact your effectiveness, your efficiency, and your profit. Depending on where you are in your build, and your current role within the organization, it can also be detrimental to your leadership, and overall health as an entrepreneur. Regular reviews of this area can help you minimize distractions that could detract from profitability.

Entrepreneur Landmine #4: Controlitis

Con-trol-i-tis (noun)

definition: a disease whereby the entrepreneur insists on maintaining total control and believing their approach is the only viable option.

thinking you are the only one who can do it right.

The tendency to handle all aspects of your business and control each function can serve entrepreneurs well during the startup phase. This can make sense in the early stages because resources may be limited, not to mention that founders often possess a deep understanding of their vision. This very hands-on approach can foster a strong sense of ownership and control in growing the business.

Until you hit the first Revenue Benchmark, from startup to $1 million, the pace of operations is often more manageable, allowing entrepreneurs to juggle multiple responsibilities. This autonomy can be financially advantageous by minimizing cost, and can make the founder feel like they're operating with speed of execution.

However, as the business begins to grow past this first Revenue Benchmark and enters a new growth phase, this behavior can become increasingly unsustainable, and even harmful to the business. Entrepreneurs who continue to insist on doing everything themselves risk becoming the bottleneck to their own growth.

Attempting to maintain total control over every aspect of the business can lead to burnout and stagnation, and even if you don't burn out, you'll miss endless opportunities. The time and energy spent on noncore tasks detract from strategic initiatives that are essential for growth and scale. As you progress through Revenue Benchmarks (discussed in the next chapter), the complexity of each new level of growth often increases, making it unrealistic for any one person to excel in every single area.

I have seen founders get away with it for a while, but eventually it will catch up. The opportunity cost of maintaining this independence becomes more and more pronounced as the business expands.

Every hour spent on routine tasks, or low-impact results, is a lost opportunity to focus on high-value results that drive growth and scale.

Be willing to let go of the need for control, and by leveraging people in your business, you can position yourself for long-term success and create a scalable, sustainable, and sellable business.

No one will care about your bottom line more than you.

So what do you need to let go of so you can focus on what will move the needle the most? Here's an approach I've used for 20 years. This is a powerful exercise that I *still* personally use every quarter. Once a quarter, I add this strategy to my State of the Union Meeting. (I break down the whole SOTU process in Chapter 7.)

It's called the DEA strategy: delegate, eliminate, automate. This process helps you identify areas where you can streamline your work, leverage others for carrying out responsibilities, simplify systems or operations with technology, or recognize where there is a need to put a process in place.

Here's how it breaks down.

D: Delegate

I can't tell you how many entrepreneurs I work with who still handle tasks such as admin, website updates, learning Facebook Ads, or funnel building. It would be far better to delegate or hire someone for those things, create a process for someone else to follow, or find a tech stack that can automate it, rather than doing everything yourself.

By leveraging the strengths of a team, you can free up time and energy to focus on high-result tasks that drive growth and innovation. Delegating tasks that are routine, time-consuming, or outside your core skills will enable you to work more efficiently and give you the ability to push the business forward.

Questions to ask if something can be delegated: Is this the best use of my time? Is there someone else I can delegate this responsibility to? Is this a high-result objective that only I can handle?

E: Eliminate

Do those networking events really have an ROI on your time? Has that partnership really been beneficial? Do you really need a rebrand even when sales aren't stable? Has that podcast or PR brought in new business? Entrepreneurs should always evaluate the ROI of each effort and be willing to eliminate anything low impact.

By streamlining and cutting out tasks that result in subpar returns, you can focus your resources on initiatives that contribute directly to growth and scalability. You have permission to adopt ruthless prioritization. Stop doing things that you don't need to do. Focus on high-result activities.

Questions to ask when considering what should be eliminated: Does this help me in achieving our largest goals? Is this necessary and needed for what we want to accomplish? Is this currently urgent and important?

A: Automate

Automation allows entrepreneurs to scale their operations without increasing their workload, enabling them to focus on strategic priorities.

By automating routine tasks such as email marketing, customer invoicing or support, social media, inventory management, and even bookkeeping and financial reporting using software platforms, tools, and technology solutions, you can increase productivity, reduce errors, *and* free up time.

Remember, the *who* should not be *you*. Your freedom is found at the intersection of more people, more processes, and more profits.

Questions to ask if something can be automated: Have I had to do this in the past? Can I create a process that someone else can follow to perform this task? Is there technology or a system I can leverage instead?

One of the best tools I've found to help with this is Trainual, a program that keeps track of delegation, training, and processes all in one place. It keeps everything documented and saves endless time. You can find out more by going to: www.candyvalentino.com/trainual

Delegate, Eliminate, Automate

For the next five days, write down all of the tasks that you do. Capture all of the tasks and activities related to your business.

TASK	DELEGATE, ELIMINATE, AUTOMATE

- **Delegate:** Take a look at the tasks and activities that you've cataloged. Is there someone on your team who can do any of these tasks at least 80% of the way that you can do it? Write that person's name in the box to the right of this task. You will be delegating this task to them.
- **Eliminate:** Take another look at your list. Are all of these tasks truly worth your time, or are some of these tasks you can totally eliminate? Note which tasks you are eliminating by writing "ELIMINATE" in the box to the right of these tasks.
- **Automate:** Take one final look at this list. Do any of these tasks have a repetitiveness that could be automated, thus saving your time for more important tasks? Note these by writing "AUTOMATE" in the box to the right of these tasks.

Feel free to carry this exercise over to a sheet of paper outside of the book, as I recognize this is likely not enough space for you to capture every task you do for your business!

By embracing delegation, elimination, and automation, entrepreneurs can avoid the pitfalls of Controlitis and start to create a path toward sustainable growth and long-term success.

Entrepreneur Landmine #5: Competency-sarcoma

Competency-sarcoma (noun)

definition: a common disease of the entrepreneur characterized by the belief of superior competency compared to their team, resulting in micromanaging tasks and projects, ultimately impeding effective delegation and team productivity.

overestimating your own abilities, leading to the belief that you must handle all tasks yourself, thereby hindering growth.

Entrepreneurship often starts with a singular vision, driven by the passion and determination of one single individual (which is likely you). More common than not, this served you and helped you acquire the level of success you currently have. But as I said in the beginning of the book, I want to challenge your thinking. The skills, talents, and habits you adopted to this point will likely not be the same ones you need to get to the next level.

As business grows, a singular vision can lead to significant pitfalls. It can cause failure within your organization as it lacks effective delegation, stifles innovation, and can undermine the potential for sustainable growth. Many founders believe that their unique vision and expertise are irreplaceable, which can lead them to micromanage every aspect of the business.

Although this may sound similar to the Controlitis entrepreneurial trap, it is different in many ways. Here are three organizational side effects of Competency-sarcoma:

Side Effect #1: Stifled Innovation. When entrepreneurs believe that their way is the only way, they inadvertently limit the creativity and problem-solving abilities of their team members. Ideas that deviate from the founder's vision are dismissed, which can result in missed opportunities for growth.

Side Effect #2: Declined Efficiency. The relentless pressure of trying to do everything themselves eventually takes its toll. They become overwhelmed and even distracted, which creates a decline in overall productivity, and can limit the organization's ability to grow with speed. Trying to wear all the hats can also start to broach the real topic of burnout. This impacts the entrepreneur's overall well-being and also affects the overall effectiveness of the business.

Side Effect #3: Risk of Stagnation. By refusing to delegate tasks or seek input from others, entrepreneurs create a bottleneck that hampers the business's ability to scale. Growth becomes stagnant as the business relies solely on the entrepreneur's limited time and resources. The founder inadvertently becomes the business's glass ceiling.

If you find yourself here, you are *not* alone. It's incredibly common for smart and capable entrepreneurs to get stuck with Competency-sarcoma because, well, you're probably very capable of doing all of these tasks on your own. But unless you want to be a one-person show, or self-employed forever, building a team around you, and developing the team so they can grow the business, is the very thing that's going to take you from a good operator to a great entrepreneur.

Here are three solutions to diminish the side effects of Competency-sarcoma:

Solution #1: Autonomous Delegation

Entrepreneurs who want to grow, and definitely those who want to scale or potentially exit, must learn Autonomous Delegation (AD), which is the act of delegating tasks to capable team members and then trusting them to execute effectively.

This empowers employees with autonomy – it not only lightens the entrepreneur's workload but also fosters a sense of trust, ownership, and accountability within the team, resulting in a more productive and capable workforce.

As a side effect, AD also fosters a team culture of continuous learning, improvement, and exploration within the organization. Acknowledging that there are multiple valid approaches to solving problems and being open to new ideas and perspectives from team members will only bring more ideas and innovation to light.

Imagine a scenario where instead of micromanaging every aspect of your business, you could trust your team to take ownership of their tasks and make decisions autonomously. That's the power of Autonomous Delegation.

It frees up your time to focus on the bigger picture. A lot of entrepreneurs are great at big-picture thinking, but the details drain the life out of them. Instead of getting bogged down in the nitty-gritty, imagine devoting your energy to strategic planning and growing your business. That's the power of AD.

Second, it empowers your team members and fosters a culture of trust and accountability. When people feel trusted to make decisions and take ownership of their work, they're more motivated and engaged. Instead of painstaking time answering the same questions every day, your employees have the tools and know what's expected of them. That's the power of AD.

Lastly, it promotes innovation and creativity within your organization. By giving your team the freedom to experiment and try new things, you're creating an environment where fresh ideas can flourish. Your growth begins to compound at light speed when you're surrounded by and collaborating with a team of talented professionals. That's the power of AD.

So how do you go about implementing Autonomous Delegation in your business? Here's a step-by-step process:

1. **Identify:** Identify tasks suitable for delegation and set clear objectives for each.
2. **Delegate:** Choose the team member(s) most capable for the task and provide necessary training and support.
3. **Define:** Set clear boundaries for autonomy and define guidelines for decision-making.
4. **Track:** Keep track of delegated tasks, offer feedback, and provide support as needed.
5. **Review:** Regularly review the delegation process, make adjustments to improve effectiveness and celebrate successes.

By implementing Autonomous Delegation in your business, and creating systemized processes to support it, you can truly empower your team and free up your own time, giving you more freedom and flexibility to drive innovation and growth. It's a win-win!

Solution #2: Systematized Processes

To get out of the trap of doing, or thinking you need to do, everything yourself, the road to getting off the hamster wheel requires systems and processes.

Systemized processes bring consistency to your operations, ensuring that tasks are done the same way each time. This consistency leads to higher-quality products or services and happier customers.

And by laying out clear steps for each task, you're cutting out any unnecessary fluff and giving your team the tools they need to work like a well-oiled machine. This means less time wasted and more productivity – not just for you, but for everyone. As your business grows, having these processes in place will make it so much easier to grow and scale at a faster pace.

But it's not just about getting things done faster – it also aids in getting things done right. Systemized processes can help minimize the risk of errors or mishaps by having established procedures and best practices. While reducing the chances of anything going wrong, whether it's a mistake on a client project or a compliance issue that could land you in hot water, you're saved endless time, money, and headaches.

Now, creating these processes might sound daunting, but it's actually pretty straightforward. Here are three tips to start:

1. **Identify:** Start by identifying the core processes in your business like sales, marketing, operations, and customer service.

2. **Document:** Next, capture and document how each core process is currently being performed. This could involve shadowing team members, interviewing key players, or even just jotting down notes on how you do things yourself.

3. **Analyze:** Once you have a good understanding of your existing processes, it's time to review and analyze them.

While you're reviewing your processes, pose questions like:
Are there any bottlenecks or inefficiencies that could be holding you back? Are there any steps in the process that can be automated or streamlined to make things run more smoothly? (You can even run the DEA Strategy on each process.) Whatever the case, aim

to standardize your procedures so that everyone knows exactly what's expected of them.

After that, it's a matter of implementation and training. Roll out the new processes to your team and answer any questions to ensure everyone is on board. Allow for questions, clarifications, and provide any necessary training or support to help them adjust to the changes.

Remember, this isn't a one-and-done kind of deal. You'll want to regularly review and update your processes to improve or change anything that's not working efficiently.

By implementing systemized processes for core business functions – as well as decision-making, project management, and communication within the business – you'll streamline your operations, and free up massive amounts of time and freedom.

Solution #3: People Capital

Your business isn't just about the products you sell or the services you offer – **it's about the people who make it all happen**. That's where People Capital comes in. It's all about investing in your employees and their potential to drive your business forward.

Here's why it's so crucial. When you prioritize your people, you're investing in your company's most valuable asset. Happy, engaged employees are more productive, more innovative, and more likely to stick around for the long haul. When you foster a positive culture and provide opportunities for growth and development, you're not just attracting top talent – you're *retaining* it.

By investing in the growth and success of team members, not only enhances their capabilities but also strengthens the overall resilience and adaptability of the business.

How can you increase People Capital in your business? Here's a step-by-step plan:

1. **Invest:** Start by investing in your employees' skills and knowledge. By offering training programs, workshops, and educational opportunities you can help them grow not just professionally, but personally, too.

2. **Reward:** Create a work environment where your employees feel valued, respected, and supported. Encourage open communication, recognize and reward achievements, and promote work-life balance.

3. **Grow:** Give your employees opportunities to advance their careers within your company. Consider career development paths, mentorship programs, or additional opportunities to take on new challenges and responsibilities.

4. **Recognize:** Your employees have lives outside of work. When they are happy and stable in their personal life, that can translate to happier, more stable employees. Encourage a healthy life overall by offering special flexibilities if or when possible, whether through scheduling, potential partial remote or hybrid work options, and time off when needed.

5. **Listen:** Finally, listen to your employees' feedback and give consideration to their thoughts and feelings. Whether it's through regular surveys, one-on-one meetings, or an open-door policy, making sure your team knows that their voices are heard and that their input is valued is important to you and your business.

By implementing these strategies, you'll be investing in your employees and building a strong foundation for your business's success. After all, when your people thrive, your business thrives. It's as simple as that!

Entrepreneur Landmine #6: Numberthritis

Numberthritis (noun)

definition: a detrimental condition caused by neglect of numerical data and financial metrics, resulting in the development of a diseased business and inefficient operations.

an affliction marked by the avoidance or dismissal of financial indicators, leading to financial disarray, instability, and death.

And finally, for the sixth entrepreneur landmine, it's the disease that's more like a plague, considering how many good entrepreneurs catch it. You can walk into every other trap I shared and still make it out alive, but this one can blow up everything.

Numberthritis, akin to its medical namesake arthritis, manifests as a debilitating condition that afflicts entrepreneurs who neglect the development of their financial skills. Just as arthritis causes stiffness and inflammation in the joints, Numberthritis stifles business progress by hindering entrepreneurs' ability to grow and sustain those levels of growth. Symptoms include a reluctance to read financial documents, an aversion to analyzing business metrics, and a general discomfort with key financial indicators.

This entrepreneurial trap ensnares business owners who procrastinate on mastering their financial acumen, who don't pay attention to their finances, won't run a cost analysis, or won't weigh opportunity cost. These activities are directly correlated to the number-one reason businesses fail: lack of profit.

However, understanding and confronting Numberthritis head on can pave the path to sustainable growth and success. Without a firm understanding of your finances, you are operating blindly, unable to make data-informed decisions – which are crucial for success. This breeds a cycle of financial instability, and can ultimately create a cash flow crisis, or worse, failure.

Businesses diseased with Numberthritis will also struggle to attract investors, secure financing, foster strategic partnerships, and will hamper their ability to scale or ever have a chance to exit.

Now, I obviously made up the word Numberthritis. So although I am speaking with tongue in cheek, there is also complete truth to everything I said. Business owners must prioritize building their financial acumen as a fundamental skill, treating it with the same urgency you may treat product development, hiring, or a new marketing and sales strategy.

Obviously, I strongly believe in delegating, eliminating, and automating roles and responsibilities, but if there was only one area in business that I feel you should play a huge role in yourself – one that you're intimately involved in – it's your finances.

Here are a few ways to increase your financial acumen and decrease the side effects of Numberthritis that may be plaguing you:

1. **Get your support.** Seek guidance and enlist the expertise of financial professionals, such as accountants, financial advisors, CFOs, and tax strategists, to help provide guidance and insights tailored to your business. Working with seasoned, experienced professionals can offer invaluable perspectives and help you navigate and understand complex financial systems. (We break down how to build your Profit Team in Chapter 9.)

2. **Build your discipline.** Commit to developing the habit of *regularly* reviewing financial documents and reports, such as income statements, balance sheets, and cash flow statements. Familiarize yourself with any CRM or POS systems reports available and understand the key financial ratios and metrics relevant to your industry. This information is invaluable in enabling you to identify cash flow trends, spot potential financial issues, and capitalize on viable opportunities for growth. (We break down in-depth how to run your State of the Union Meeting in Chapter 7.)

3. **Leverage your technology.** You don't have to go at this alone. Deploy financial software solutions designed to simplify and streamline the tracking and analysis of data. Leveraging accounting software, business intelligence technology, and dashboard analytics will empower you to gain real-time visibility into your financial health and will help you understand your finances better so you can make more informed decisions.

4. **Increase your knowledge.** Find resources, courses, workshops, and programs dedicated to building financial intelligence for entrepreneurs. There are online and in-person events, business schools focused on business finance, and mentorship programs that provide important education on understanding financial documents, interpreting KPIs, and even helping you navigate through learning cost analysis, evaluating sunk cost, and how certain expenses like opportunity cost don't show up on your financial reports.

This education helps you make better data-driven decisions. And as we know, the better our decisions, the better our reality. For more information on our programs and the ways we help entrepreneurs with their financial acumen, go to **www.candyvalentino .com**.

I know that financial data can make even the most experienced and enthusiastic entrepreneur's eyes glaze over. But mastering your financial acumen is not a luxury. It is truly a necessity for long-term success.

Numberthritis, the silent killer of businesses, thrives on ignorance and procrastination but can easily be defeated. By making a concerted effort to prioritize your financial education, embrace available technology, develop the habit of building awareness, and seek the guidance of professionals you can confront Numberthritis head on and get on a course toward sustainable, scalable growth.

Now, regardless which of these landmines you've stepped on, there is no shame or guilt here. Neither of those emotions will serve you. What will is the understanding that no one is born with this knowledge, yet building it is completely within your control.

Your ability to build a scalable, sustainable, and sellable business will depend on your ability to overcome any of these landmines you may have stepped on, and will require you to start believing what's true: **you are fully capable of building the business you want, and you're undoubtedly worthy of everything you desire.**

So now that that's out of the way, let's start building.

CHAPTER 3

Creating a Scalable, Sustainable, and Sellable Business

Unless you want to work forever, you need to build a business that generates revenue and creates wealth so you can actually achieve what you truly want – FREEDOM.

After I concluded my second exit, I started sharing some business tips on social media. I had been nauseated by some of the information I saw online, and what I heard that was shared. It was obvious which of these "experts" were in the first few years of their first business, or had never built a real business at all, compared to how you converse with those who built a scalable, sustainable, and sellable model with people, processes, and of course the holy grail, profit.

I genuinely wasn't sure if anyone would care to hear about, or learn about, financial reporting, understanding your numbers, how to evaluate data, and measure KPIs – I mean, who wants to get real and hear the truth these days? So I was quite shocked to find out that some people did.

Often, the truth can hurt like a mother. Sometimes it's not fun, and quite frankly it can suck sometimes. But as hard as it might be to hear, the truth is just the truth and if we don't attach a negative feeling of guilt or shame to it, we can see it for what it is – just the truth and that it's not a reflection of your worth, your intelligence, or your abilities. We don't know what we don't know. But once we *do* know, it's what we do with it that matters.

The worst thing you can do is live in denial. Ignorance may be bliss, but avoidance is death. So if throughout this chapter you start to identify some areas that need improvement, don't stress about it. You're here for a reason and what you do *next* is all that matters.

Regardless of whether you've been avoiding your numbers, neglecting your finances, or just numbing out to it all, I promise you that all roads to more revenue, more profit, and more freedom will run through numbers. Whether it's a KPI, a metric, or a financial number on your P&L, numbers and data are the keys to business success.

Time and time again, I have helped entrepreneurs and business owners understand these numbers, leverage their knowledge, and grow their businesses – and if you're willing to do the work, I'd be honored to help you, too. Numbers – as opposed to opinions – are honest. They are true in form and when you understand their language, numbers and data can show you the path to achieve every business goal you desire.

The fastest way to have clarity on the next strategic moves you should make in your business is to have accurate knowledge of where your business stands. And regardless of whether you're currently in growth or you're in scale, your business still lives and dies on its profit.

Most well-intended entrepreneurs full of dreams, grit, and ambition can find their way to generating millions of dollars in revenue, but 91% of them are also proficient in losing millions of dollars – ultimately costing them their entire business, savings, and dreams (and sometimes their families) because they didn't master how to *keep* millions of dollars in profit.

Remember this saying: "Revenue is vanity, profit is sanity, and cash is king." No matter how old that saying is, it still rings true today.

The Foundation of Financial Success

When I learned the stat that more than 9 out of every 10 businesses fail financially, I can honestly say that I have never wondered why. It's pretty easy to see.

We aren't taught about money in school, college teaches us to go into massive debt in hopes of a payoff down the road, and then there is this constant focus on revenue and sales. And yes, acquiring customers is the key in business growth, and sales revenue is the foundation. But substantial growth can actually kill your business.

I know that doesn't seem possible, but it is. I have seen it numerous times and am reminded about David, a client this very thing happened to. David mastered the skill of acquiring customers, understood his target market, and generated millions of dollars in sales. He started from nothing, built his business from the ground up, and was consistently growing his top-line revenue every year.

The challenge was that as David's revenue grew, so did his spending. He started experimenting with new ways to market and advertise, he hired support staff to help with his workflow, and he added new products and services to his offerings, and his expenses grew.

A year went by with this pattern. He went to file his taxes, only to realize that although his revenue increased, his net income decreased. He barely had enough to pay his employees the next quarter. How was this possible? Because although David had sales, he lacked profit.

Having built his business from the ground up, David had an intimate knowledge of who his customer was and what they needed, which gave him a leg up on that one singular business growth mechanism – customer acquisition. But he didn't increase his financial acumen and didn't understand how to *keep* more of that money. **Revenue is how you build a business; profit is how you sustain a business.**

Most founders think they add more sales and the rest will take care of itself. If only that were true.

Financial challenges occur most commonly when one or two things happen in your business: sales drastically increase, or sales drastically decrease. You would think only the latter would be true. But when sales increase at a rapid pace, there can still be challenges.

Imagine you woke up one day and decided to build your dream house. You dreamed of this beautiful sprawling ranch house with 12-foot ceilings and a big open family room. You had the architect carefully lay out the plans so that the master bedroom was on one side of the house, and the guest bedrooms were on the other, with the kitchen and family room located perfectly in between. Since it was a ranch house, you didn't need to dig a basement, so you just poured a slab. Once the slab was poured, the framing began, then the roof, then the walls, followed by plumbing, electrical, HVAC, drywall, and so on. After the house was fully finished, you moved in. You and your spouse have been living in it for a couple years now, and decide you want an even bigger house. So you hire a contractor to build another floor on top of your roof. They start laying the floor, adding framing, walls, more electrical, more plumbing, more HVAC, more drywall. Do you think that house is going to be stable? Do you think that a structure built for one floor will support a two-story house?

Of course not! It would crumble before it was even complete. Now, thankfully, there are laws and building codes that prevent this sort of thing from happening to houses and other commercial property, but in business, there are no such laws. So anyone can just increase sales, generate more revenue, and add more customers. The challenge is that, like the house, the structure you built will not sustain that expansion any more than that slab built for a ranch house will support a two-story mansion.

You have to pause, reimagine the house, redesign the plans, and remove some of the components. You have to take time to dig the footers, lay the foundation, and rebuild the structure to support the new growth and changes. If you blow past that pause point and start building up and out, more likely than not, the whole thing will crash down. The same is true in business. If your income or sales grow significantly, at the same rate, so do your expenses. One great month, quarter, or even year can deceive you.

If you achieve new benchmarks of revenue and blow past key Pause Points in your growth, the very thing you think you want could be the very thing that causes your failure.

More revenue, more growth, more sales, a bigger business, a bigger team, or a larger footprint does not guarantee more profit. The revenue-focused, growth-only mindset is a threat to your business and to your overall sustainability. If you want to get away from feeling like you're throwing things against the wall to see what sticks, or the feeling like you're on the perpetual entrepreneurial hamster wheel, you have to master understanding profitability.

One fundamental business principle to remember is knowing that you don't have to leave your success to chance. You can avoid the fate of the 91% of entrepreneurs whose businesses fail in the first 10 years. By implementing a few core functions in your business, you'll not only build a strong foundation for your business's success, but you'll create a scalable, sustainable, and sellable machine that becomes unshakable in the face of challenge.

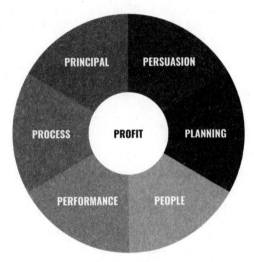

Seven Core Functions of a Scalable, Sustainable, and Sellable Business

As a serial entrepreneur with over two and a half decades of hands-on experience, I've had the privilege of being in the trenches witnessing firsthand the challenges of business. From startups growing to their first $1 million in revenue to thriving enterprises generating $250 million in revenue, I've uncovered recurring patterns that separate the successful 9% from the rest.

This foundational framework represents the culmination of extensive research and analysis conducted on small and mid-sized businesses across various industries. From in-depth interviews, case studies, and surveys of real business owners, I was able to gain a comprehensive understanding of the challenges and opportunities entrepreneurs face. Through this research, plus my own experience, I've identified patterns that transcend industry boundaries.

By leveraging data and observations, I've crafted an approach that gets to the bottom of what it actually takes to build a thriving, scalable, and sustainable business.

If you want to know what truly matters in your business, this framework will serve as a roadmap. Any entrepreneur looking to navigate the complexities of building a business with confidence and clarity will need to consider these seven fundamental functions of a powerful business:

1. **Profits:** The core financial function in your business. This applies to managing revenue, controlling costs, and ultimately maximizing profitability. Understanding financial statements, cash flow management, and financial forecasting are all essential aspects of this foundation.

2. **People:** The core team and employee function in your business. Any successful business heavily relies on its people – the team and employees. Building a talented, motivated, and cohesive team is crucial for achieving business goals. This foundation encompasses hiring the right individuals, fostering a positive company culture, providing training and development opportunities, and effective leadership.

3. **Persuasion:** The core role of sales and marketing in your business – all the components that involve persuading potential customers to buy your products or services, and effectively communicating your value proposition. Sales strategies, marketing campaigns, branding, and customer relationship management are key components of this foundation.

4. **Planning:** The core role of strategic planning in your business. It plays a vital role in guiding the direction and growth of your business. It involves setting clear goals, defining strategies to achieve

those goals, and regularly reviewing and adjusting plans based on the market and factors. This foundation encompasses market analysis, competitive positioning, product development, and resource allocation.

5. **Processes:** The core role of processes and systems in your business. This foundation involves designing and implementing effective workflows, standard operating procedures, and deploying technology solutions to improve productivity, minimize errors, and enhance customer and employee satisfaction.

6. **Performance:** The core role of performance and optimization in your business. This foundation focuses on measuring key performance indicators (KPIs), analyzing data to gain insights, and implementing strategies to enhance business performance. This includes aspects such as sales performance, operational efficiency, customer satisfaction, and employee productivity – each critical for long-term success.

7. **Principal:** The core role of the entrepreneur, founder, CEO. This foundation emphasizes the importance of strong leadership, strategic decision-making, and overall health of the leader. It involves embodying fundamentals such as vision setting, problem-solving, decision-making, and effective communication.

Although there are seven core competencies entrepreneurs need to master, the first – profit – is the center of it all, because without profit, you're dead on arrival. You can't focus on the other six without it. You can't hire more people, because profitability provides the financial resources needed to offer competitive salaries, benefits, and incentives to attract and retain top talent. You won't be able to increase your sales and marketing efforts, because profit fuels sales and marketing initiatives. It provides the budget for advertising, promotions, and branding activities. Without it, you can't invest in acquiring new customers, which will limit your ability to drive sales and grow.

I could go on but you get the point. Profit is the lifeblood to your business. And although talking about profitability, cash flow management, financial forecasting, and cost analysis might seem like another language, profit is very simple. By tradition and definition, profit is what's left over from sales revenue after you've covered your expenses. However, this very traditional approach to profit could be what's keeping you from chasing more revenue instead of focusing on obtaining more profit.

Traditional accounting practices have been around for hundreds of years. The way most professionals look at accounting has also been the same for hundreds of years. And yet 9 out of 10 businesses fail, which made me wonder if there is an alternative way to look at it.

There is. Something about the philosophy of "grow your revenue, reduce expenses, and keep the remaining profit" simply doesn't work – especially when there aren't any profits to keep.

Let's break down each part of that philosophy and reframe them.

Grow Your Revenue

We often hear that revenue is king. It's not. Even though revenue is important, here's the thing: not all revenue is equal. Because it's not just about how much money is coming in; it's about where it's coming from and how much you get to keep at the end of the day.

So before we "grow your revenue," we first must recognize that not all revenue is created equal. If you don't regularly evaluate and measure the return on your effort, whether it's marketing efforts, revenue by employee, advertising efforts, revenue by hour, or profitability by service or product (there are endless metrics you can evaluate), you have no way to know what's working. Knowing what's working, and what isn't, *before* you attempt to grow your revenue can save you so much time and money.

When working directly with clients (this is particularly effective with service-based, B2B, or DTC businesses), one of my favorite analyses to start with is performing a quarterly customer profitability analysis. If you haven't ever measured this in the past and you choose to execute this, and this is all you get out of this book, you just easily increased your investment a thousandfold.

Let's start by breaking down your revenue sources into different categories. Maybe you have different product lines, serve different types of customers, or sell through various channels. Once you've got them sorted, take a hard look at each one.

Figure out how much it costs you to generate that revenue and how much you're actually making from it. This helps you see which parts of your business are the real money-makers and others that might be dragging you down. You can do this regardless of what kind of business you have.

All businesses sell something, create revenue, and have customers. But not all customers are created equal, either. Some might make big one-time purchases, while others come back time and time again. Understanding your customers, where and how you acquired them, and knowing the lifetime value of your customers is key. This gives you the ability to look beyond the initial sale and helps you figure out how much a customer is worth to your business over the long term. Once you know who your high-value customers are, you can focus your efforts on keeping them happy and attracting more like them.

Performing a customer profitability analysis is straightforward. And the numbers you get from this analysis show you a path toward greater profitability. You may have business tools to do this, but here's a summary:

1. **Segment customers:** Divide your customer base into distinct segments based on relevant characteristics such as demographics, purchasing behavior, or geographic location. You can use your CRM or POS system reports to help.

2. **Calculate segment profitability:** Determine the profitability of each of those customer segments by analyzing revenue generated, associated costs, and contribution margins. This allows you to identify segments that contribute significantly to overall profit and those that do not. This may identify which segments need to be adjusted, refined, or eliminated to improve profitability.

3. **Customer acquisition cost (CAC):** Calculate the cost of acquiring customers within each segment. Factor your marketing and advertising expenses, any sales commissions, and other costs.

4. **Retention and loyalty analysis:** Evaluate retention rates and loyalty of customers within each segment. Identify which of the segments have the highest customer retention.

Now, the fun part:

5. **Optimization:**
   - Sort your customers from most profitable to least profitable.

- How much revenue does the least profitable category represent? What's similar about the most profitable? How were they acquired? What are their buying habits?

- What steps would you have to take to eliminate the least profitable customers? How many of the most profitable customers would you have to acquire to replace that revenue?

- How much profit would be gained if you replaced the least profitable clients with the most profitable ones?

- Based on the insights you gained, how can you develop and refine tailored marketing strategies to acquire more of your most profitable clients? How can you maximize profitability within each segment?

6. **Compare CAC (customer acquisition cost) to the CLV (customer lifetime value)** in each segment as well as the loyalty and retention rates to determine the effectiveness of your marketing and sales efforts. This process will yield long-term profitability that will create substantial stability in your operations.

In the end, it's all about focusing on the bottom line. But by taking a closer look at where your revenue is coming from and how profitable it really is, you can make better, more informed data-driven decisions about where to invest your time and resources.

It's not always about chasing the biggest numbers; sometimes smaller, more consistent streams of revenue can make all the difference in the world.

Reduce Expenses

We can do that. And I'll talk about how to do exactly that later in the book, but before we do, I want to flip the script on this. What if we instead find expenses that could create profit? I know that might sound like a miracle straight from the Bible when Jesus walked on water, but hear me out. It's not just *possible*; it can drastically change your bottom line.

I've done this a lot personally, especially in my last couple of businesses. At first it wasn't intentional; it was purely out of frustration. I was holding my monthly State of the Union Meeting (I break this down in Chapter 7), and while reviewing my profit-and-loss statement, I hated seeing all of the expenses related to generating social content. From videographers to editors to graphic designers to the people who post it, it was frustrating to me that I had such a high expense without a significant ROI. On top of that, it took a significant amount of time because the quality wasn't where I needed it to be. So out of frustration I decided, "I'm not doing this anymore." And instantly I thought, "We can't be the only ones having this challenge. How can we hire everyone in-house and then offset this expense by selling a high-quality content creation service to the entrepreneurs we work with?" And what was once an expense became profit. And then a light bulb moment happened as I thought, "Can I do that for these other expenses?"

Let's start with a simple concept and pose this question: Which expenses in your business could potentially become a profit center? Perhaps it's not clear cut, so just think about it. What are you currently spending money on that could perhaps generate revenue *and* reduce your expenses simultaneously if you imagined it in another way?

Another example of this is a lumber mill I frequently visited in Pennsylvania. The mill would cut and sell all kinds of lumber, beams, and posts, in any length, different species, custom widths, you name it. When doing renovations or building commercial buildings, I would get my lumber from this mill because it had the widest selection. They had everything and could get anything I needed. When I visited the mill to pick out something special, I always made sure I wore flat boots (not the cute kind) because there was always tons of sawdust on the floor.

One day while I was there and looking at the large piles of sawdust everywhere, I heard the loud sound of a backup beeper to my right and quickly stepped out of the way. Just then a skid loader blew past me and started scooping the sawdust. I asked the owner, "What do you do with all of that sawdust?"

"I pay my guys to move it to the other property and then we either have to dispose of it or sometimes we burn it; it just depends how much is here. Why do you ask?" he asked, smiling and letting out a half chuckle.

"Can I buy it from you?"

"Buy it? You can have it, but what on earth are you going to do with it?"

"Remember that wood I just got from you for the barn renovation project at the animal sanctuary?"

"Yes. . ." he said inquisitively.

"We currently *buy* sawdust for the animals' bedding. Since you said you'd give it to me, can I pay you to deliver it the next time you're out by the farm?"

"Sure!" he said excitedly.

That sawdust saved the animal sanctuary about $2,000 a year in expenses. For the lumber mill, it changed from an expense of *paying* to dispose of sawdust, to *getting paid* to deliver sawdust. Of course, they had more sawdust than we could ever use, and they started selling it to other places in the area, creating a revenue stream that was once an expense. *That* is a double win.

What's your sawdust? Do you have any by-products or underutilized resources?

Amazon mastered this when they launched Amazon Web Services. AWS started as a cost center for Amazon and their need for massive data storage capabilities. Their own need for something that would have been an expense turned into a multi-billion-dollar enterprise that became more profitable than their original business model, today generating 70% of the company's total profit.[1]

How can you leverage the expenses in your business? Here are a handful of ways to rewire your thinking and start to look at expenses differently.

Do you invest in data-analysis tools and personnel to understand your customer behavior, market trends, and operational efficiencies? These could be packaged and sold as a service to other businesses looking to improve their operations or make data-driven decisions.

Do you have any unused space, or can you leverage your physical space in another way? Take a look at your business to see if there is any excess office space, or warehouse space, perhaps consider renting out or subleasing the space to other businesses.

Businesses often invest in developing expertise or intellectual property for their operations. This could be proprietary software, patented technologies, or specialized knowledge. Take a look at your services or processes and see if there are any assets that can be licensed or even sold to other businesses operating in related fields.

If your business invests in employee training programs to enhance skills and knowledge, look to see if you can potentially offer these programs to other businesses, whether as a service or by licensing the training materials.

Businesses that consume significant amounts of energy might invest in renewable energy sources such as solar panels or wind turbines. Look to see if the excess energy generated could be sold back to the grid or to other businesses.

If your business owns specialized equipment or machinery that is not in constant use, you could rent it out to other businesses or individuals. Businesses with efficient logistics and distribution networks could look to offer their services to other companies; businesses that collect customer data for internal use could explore ethical opportunities to aggregate or sell this data.

I am not suggesting you change your business model and add a bunch of these things into your offerings without doing a cost analysis first. What I am suggesting is to simply look at your top expenses and brainstorm possible ways to self-liquidate, create profit from, or even offset some of their costs. By looking at the same things in a new way and just posing the question, we are enforcing the habit of seeing more opportunities where others may see only obstacles.

Remember innovative thinking, and a new approach, can potentially turn a traditional business expense into a revenue-generating opportunity.

Keep Remaining Profit

To be left with any remaining profit to keep, we have to deduct an endless list of expenses. The direct costs associated with producing or acquiring the products or services sold by the business is called COGS (Cost of Goods Sold) and can include the cost of materials, labor directly involved in production, and manufacturing overhead. You deduct any ongoing expenses incurred in regular business operations such as rent, utilities, insurance, salaries and wages, marketing expenses, insurance, office supplies, equipment, and/or maintenance. If the business has loans from borrowed money, interest expenses on those funds or lines of credit are deducted from revenue. Once you deduct all of that from revenue, and anything else I didn't name, you arrive at the profit.

At the beginning of this section I said that there was something about the philosophy of Revenue – Expenses = Keep Remaining Profit that simply doesn't seem to work, especially when there aren't any profits to keep.

So I posed the question of whether there was a better way. What if instead of paying all your expenses to see what's left over to keep, you take an average percentage of profit out of your revenue to pay yourself and then pay expenses with what's left? Instead of

$$Revenue - Expenses = Profit$$

we use the formula

$$Revenue - Profit = Expenses$$

By implementing this methodology, you essentially create a simple budget for your business in order to guarantee you earn some profit on your efforts. This approach also builds the habits of expense reduction and understanding how to apply cost allocations without having to learn a bunch of financial principles.

Many entrepreneurs fail to grasp the significance of budgeting and adopt a mentality of just covering expenses without thorough analysis, assuming that the expenditure will eventually yield a return. Unfortunately, this approach often leads to financial instability and the eventual demise of the business.

This change in philosophy also allows you to step off the perpetual tax write-off wheel so that you can make better decisions about purchases and investments you make into the business.

So often I see entrepreneurs spending $10,000, $20,000, $100,000 or more on something they don't need in order to save $2,500 in taxes. Flipping the formula gives a way to ask better questions and be more mindful about what expenses to take on. "Does the business need this?" "Is there a better solution, or an alternative solution?" "Is there a better time to make this purchase?"

Although there are great benefits with this approach, there are also some potential drawbacks. The first is that prioritizing short-term profits can diminish potential future gains. Consistently withdrawing excessive profits without reinvesting adequately in the business can hinder its long-term growth potential. The second is that when profits are continually withdrawn without strategic reinvestment, it can stifle the business's capacity to expand and grow. The third is that using this model can become more complex to align for those who have business partners and investors.

The key is to balance proper percentages of immediate profit with strategic long-term business investment. Even if you're currently in a financial position where profits from your business are not immediately needed, I want to encourage you to establish the habit of setting aside profit, because the lack of it is the number-one reason businesses fail. This practice fosters financial discipline and prevents you from relying solely on future cash flow, debt, or other income streams.

When you prioritize profit and base your financial decisions on your current capabilities rather than on future aspirations, you keep focus on what matters most. By doing so, profit is less likely to be overlooked or neglected, which will help you start to stack the odds in your favor of becoming part of the 9% – and help you get one step closer to building a scalable, sustainable, and perhaps even sellable business.

What the Numbers Are Saying

I'll never forget the first time I learned a hard lesson about profit firsthand in real time building a business. I was sitting in my accountant's office at the little round table she had in the corner. I was only 21 or 22 years old at the time. She was going over my financials and showing me the revenue and profit against my projections and reviewing what next year's forecasts were based on these numbers. I was so happy to see on paper what I knew all along that year: my business was continuing to grow.

I was able to hire more staff, and advertise in a bigger way. I started to look for new locations to acquire and was even able to pay myself. I had even paid off the SBA loan I got to start my business. She took her pen and pointed to one number on the page and said, "You even had $103,000 in profit." I was so excited. Yet at the very same moment, my mind flipped to my business bank account. I looked up from the number on the 1120s form right where her pen was pointed and said, "Wait. How is that possible? I only have $30,000 in the bank." I think she tried not to laugh. Thankfully, I never take myself too seriously so I was the one who laughed as soon as the words left my mouth. Although accounting is generally looking at what happened after it happened, I knew there was nothing wrong with her calculations, so there had to be something with mine. "Just because you show the profit, doesn't mean you have the cash," she said. "Oh," I said. That's about all I could say. "Candy, your profits are even better than the industry average, it's somewhere around 10%," she said. "You're doing great!" she added.

I smiled, thanked her for the kindness, and wrote out my tax checks to the IRS, the state, and the local governments for their due. Then I drove back to my office and made a vow that I would never let that happen again.

That moment put me on a warpath to figure out the science of business. I was committed to increasing my financial acumen, understanding my financial reports, becoming fluent in the language of numbers and business finance, and learning how to be an avid listener and interrupter to the data that talks to us in our business – and by all means to relentlessly figure out how to keep more of the money I made, because 10% wasn't going to cut it.

I know with certainty if that girl with no business degree, no corporate background, and no money could figure out how to make more revenue, keep more profit, and create more freedom, then you can, too.

But here's the deal: you can't fix what you don't face. Your finances are for you. No one will care about your money more than you, and no one should. Having your finger on the financial pulse of your business is not just a priority for each and every entrepreneur, it's a necessity.

Learning this, understanding this, and knowing how to implement it is going to be the most powerful thing you can do, and the good news is – you're going to.

Remember, you've figured out lots of things before. In fact, you've done hard things, survived hard things, overcome hard things. Learning some numbers is nothing compared to that.

Profit isn't merely about numbers on a spreadsheet – it's about what profit enables you to do. It gives you the cash to invest in new ideas and to develop better products, and it fuels growth, sparks innovation, and gives you the ability to reach more customers.

Profit is also a litmus test for how well your business is doing. It tells you if you're running things efficiently or if there are areas that need to be tweaked. By evaluating profit, you can spot critical problems early on and make necessary adjustments to keep your business on track. In the last part of the book, "More Freedom NOW," I talk more about this and how profit plays a *huge* role in whether or not your business will ever be sellable.

Remember, profit isn't just about the health of the business – it's also about people. It's what allows you to pay your employees fairly, hire exceptional talent, and foster a positive culture. When your business is profitable, everyone truly wins.

And let's not forget, it's also about stability. Profit acts as a safety net, protecting your business from unexpected challenges. With healthy profit, you can weather the storms that will inevitably come your way and will enable you to come out stronger on the other side.

When your business is profitable, you have the power to do more than just make money – you can make an impact. Whether you're supporting your community or investing in causes you care about, profit gives you the ability to make the world a better place.

CHAPTER 4

Real-World Revenue Growth

Success in business is determined by your ability to acquire new customers and retain them for the long term.

I don't know where the myth originates from, but there is a widely spread misconception that the global mega company McDonald's doesn't make a profit on cheeseburgers alone.

While it's true that some items on their menu are strategically priced to attract customers, and subsequently do have lower profit margins, McDonald's still makes a profit on their cheeseburgers.

Even though McDonald's is very much in the real estate business – it owns one of the largest real estate empires in the world – they are still very much in the food and franchise business, collecting more than $25 billion in revenue in 2023 alone. Although they collected $7.3 billion in rental income, they still need to flip burgers because if their franchises were to fail, McDonald's would fail. Still, there is a lot to learn from how they employ a sophisticated pricing and menu strategy that considers both individual item profitability and the overall spending patterns of their customers.

While the profit on a single cheeseburger is currently less than five cents, when they ask customers to add fries and a drink, it significantly boosts the overall profitability of each transaction. Fries and drinks are far more significant, with soft drinks having 90% profit. This makes combo meals the backbone of their model and why they're heavily promoted by employees and tracked by the company.

A cornerstone of McDonald's profitability lies in its ability to upsell and cross-sell. Like many other billion-dollar business giants, they have mastered the understanding of this simple yet profound business principle: **it will always cost you more to acquire a new customer than it will to get an existing one to buy more from you.**

I see newer entrepreneurs confuse revenue versus profit, just as growth versus scale is often misunderstood. Revenue is the amount of money your business brings in from selling its products or services. Profit is the money that your business actually gets to keep after covering all of its costs.

Growth is the process of increasing revenue, expanding your customer base, or adding new products or services, whereas scaling is about taking that growth and making it sustainable and efficient. It's the magic potion that allows your business to become larger without needing more resources. Scaling is when you increase your capability without a proportional increase in resources or costs, thus becoming more profitable.

It's the difference between being rich from earned income as opposed to having wealth from assets. The latter is more subdued, calmer, quieter – but it's actually what you want. The same applies when comparing newer entrepreneurs trying to grow by selling you every product, service, or program on getting more, more, more customers. Compare that to seasoned, experienced founders who advise you to pause at specific points, develop an acquisition strategy, build a customer profile, maximize the revenue of those existing customers, maintain profitability – and *then* scale strategically. This can result in finding more customers with profiles like our best customers so we can do more with less.

Regardless of whether you have a local brick-and-mortar or an online store, an e-commerce business, or a service-based business, you can grow your revenue and increase profitability by leveraging the same timeless, proven business strategies that billion-dollar companies like McDonald's deploy.

And while many entrepreneurs think that growing their revenue comes from acquiring new customers, *you* know that maximizing the revenue from your existing customers is a significantly better strategy. So let's break down how to do exactly that.

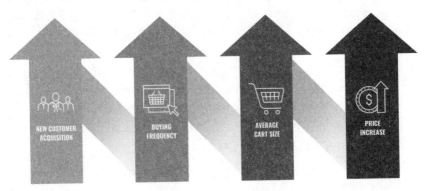

Average Order Value (AOV)

What companies like McDonald's and many other large successful businesses do well is their consistent ability to increase each customer's average order value by cross-selling or upselling other products and/or services.

McDonald's does it through their focus on combo meals, Starbucks does it through pastry and breakfast foods, Apple does it through their higher-priced models and add-ons like AppleCare, Sephora does it by offering product sets and limited-edition collections, and online businesses do it through endless order bumps with OTOs (one-time offers): "But wait, there's more!"

Here are nine ways you can boost revenue and profitability achieving a greater AOV:

Upselling: Suggest higher-value or additional items that complement your customer's current selection. This could be offering a larger size of something, or a premium version of something you offer.

Bundling: Offer bundle deals, or packages of products or services that enable customers to purchase complementary products together at a slightly discounted price. This encourages customers to add more items to their cart or can even get them to try a product or service they wouldn't otherwise have purchased on their own.

Cross-selling: Recommend related or complementary products at the point of sale. For instance, if a customer is buying coffee, suggest a pastry, coffee cake, or take-home coffee. Use cross-selling with upselling; for example, when a customer orders a medium coffee, you let them know they can get double for just $0.50 more. So they buy an extra-large coffee instead and *then* add on a scone and coffee cake. A more advanced way to cross-sell utilizing technology is to leverage your customers' purchase history or browsing behavior to personalize cross-selling recommendations.

Minimum order thresholds for free shipping: Customers will spend more to get free shipping and are willing to add more items to their cart to avoid paying shipping fees, which will increase their average order value. Consider setting a minimum order value that is higher than your current average order value for customers to qualify for free shipping.

Volume and bulk discounts: Offer discounts or special pricing for larger-quantity purchases. This encourages customers to buy more of the same product or service, or to try additional products or services you offer. Another example, if applicable to your business, is implementing a tiered pricing structure where the individual product or service price decreases as the quantity ordered increases.

Limited-time offers and promotions: Create urgency and scarcity by incentivizing larger purchases with limited-time offers and promotions. There's the infamous "Buy one, get one free" strategy or "Spend X amount, get Y% off," or my personal favorite, which served me for 20-plus years in various businesses and is much more effective: "Spend X amount, get Y amount free."

I learned this from L Brands (formerly the Limited Corporation). They are the parent company for brands like Express, Victoria's Secret, and Bath & Body Works, to name a few. They ran with this slight change in the limited-time offer promotion structure and it resulted in billions of dollars in sales revenue over more than 30 years.

Lastly, always have an expiration date on your limited-time offers. I don't think the word "always" works very well in business, but this is a case that "always" might apply. Flash sales, promotions, special offers – creating urgency – works best to encourage customers to make impulsive purchases or stock up on items when there is a time limit to do so.

Loyalty programs: Who doesn't love a good loyalty program? Customers love them, and businesses of all sizes do, too. Quite simply, they work. Implement a loyalty program where your customers earn points or rewards based on their purchase amount. Rewards can vary from discounts or free products to exclusive perks for reaching certain spending thresholds. This encourages retention, fosters increased buying frequency, and can increase average order value by rewarding loyal customers with incentives and discounts.

If done right, customers will tout their loyalty badge with pride, making sure it's known they are a card-carrying American Airlines Concierge Key who can board their flight before everyone else and a proud Titanium Marriott Bonvoy Member who gets room upgrades and free breakfast all over the globe.

Personalized recommendations: When possible, using data analytics and machine learning algorithms to analyze customer preferences and behavior can result in significant revenue and profitability by providing personalized product recommendations based on past purchases, browsing history, or demographic information. This enables you to tailor marketing messages, email campaigns, and special offers to specific customers or customer segments to encourage higher-value and/or more frequent purchases.

Add-ons and accessories: Offer add-on products or accessories that complement the main purchase. If you've ever bought a TV or other electronics at Best Buy or Target, you know you get hit with the "Do you want to buy an extended electronic warranty?" question. As annoying as that may be to you or me, industry studies show that over 42% of consumers opt to take one – which is why you now find many businesses offering extended warranties on everything from TVs to phones to speakers to lamps!

But it doesn't stop there. Highlighting the benefits of purchasing the add-on products and accessories for each order will increase your average order value overall. That TV needs an HDMI cable, a sound bar, and a special electronic cleaner, not to mention that every iPhone needs a case and four extra plugs, chargers, and dongles. You have to have an extra for the car, office, kitchen, *and* bedroom (plus you know you lose one the first time your kid asks to borrow a charger!). Encourage customers to save time and buy add-ons and accessories right at the time of their order.

Here's the thing. If you read all of this thinking that you haven't been paying attention to metrics like these, you're not alone. When I started my work with entrepreneurs, I was shocked how many were doing $3 million, $5 million, $10 million-plus in revenue yet didn't know how they acquired their customers, what their customers were spending on average, how frequently customers were buying from them, or what their lifetime customer value was to the company.

Regardless of whether you love or hate McDonald's, business owners of all sizes can learn from their model of maximizing revenue from each customer and how they use multiple levers to remain profitable through every economic, market, or global situation change. With their approach to combining strategic pricing, product variety, and focus on operational efficiency, McDonald's successfully maximizes profitability across its entire product offering, including the iconic cheeseburger.

So, can you build a business *without* any of this knowledge? Sure. But man, just imagine how successful you'd be if you built it *with* this knowledge!

Calculating AOV:

Formula: AOV = Total Revenue / Total Number of Orders

Example: $45,000 in sales from 5,000 orders results in an AOV of $9

Remember, your AOV can also be called "average cart" or "average ticket," depending on the industry you're in. The formula is the same. This critical KPI shows how much each of your customers spends on average per transaction.

And look, it's not like I started my first company knowing any of this, either. To quote Alicia Silverstone in the 1990s hit movie *Clueless*, "As if!"

However, I was fortunate enough to be around founders and business owners in my early 20s who lived and breathed business metrics. Most of them were twice my age, and had companies 10 times the size of mine at the time, so I modeled what they did and picked up this behavior. Once I adopted the behavior and saw the difference in my revenue, profit, and overall stability (and sanity), I made it a habit.

Once I had the consistent habit of evaluating metrics like these, I started to identify patterns. Some customers were coupon queens, some were quarterly buyers, some we only saw for their birthday scratch-off (insanely successful promo we ran for 15 years), some waited to get a gift card for Christmas, some we saw every four to six weeks, and some were cultlike customers who visited frequently and told everyone they knew about us.

I began to wonder if there was a way to find more of these cultlike customers. Where did the ones we had come from, so we could find more like them? That's when I posed this question: Can I reverse engineer our customer acquisition strategy and acquire more customers like these?

The answer is a resounding *yes*. But wait, there's more! (*in my infomercial voice*).

Before I get into the process of architecting your customer acquisition strategy, increasing your average order value is not the *only* way to create *More Revenue NOW*.

The sister concept to increasing your AOV is increasing buying frequency.

When I think about globally recognized companies and brands we all know, and review those that have done this exceptionally well, my mind can't help but go instantly to Amazon. I spoke about them in Chapter 3 when we discussed companies that successfully took the approach of turning an expense into profit.

Since I would bet that you use Amazon on at least a monthly basis at minimum, you are familiar with their "helpful tools" that save time for their customers and thus increase buying frequency for their company. Amazon's Prime membership program not only offers customers benefits such as free two-day shipping, access to streaming services like Prime Video, and exclusive deals and discounts, but it gives them monthly recurring revenue (MRR). Prime membership customers make more purchases on Amazon than non-Prime members.

Their Subscribe & Save program allows customers to subscribe to recurring automatic delivery of everyday essentials and in turn be rewarded with a discount. This format encourages more frequent purchases (often before the customer needs the item) while citing "convenience and ease" for the shopper.

The e-commerce behemoth also utilizes sophisticated algorithms to personalize product recommendations based on the customer's browsing and purchase history, added the "One-Click Ordering" feature, allowing purchases with a single click, and streamlined the checkout process that leads to more frequent transactions. Amazon hosts annual events like Prime Day, Black Friday, and Cyber Monday. These support sales in multiple ways: increased buying frequency, advertising significant deals to attract new customers to their membership, and creating a sense of urgency for customers to make purchases more frequently and spend more because they are buying at a discount.

Alternatively, when we step out of e-commerce and look to brick-and-mortar stores, we can look at the coffee juggernaut Starbucks and their approach to increased buying frequency. Some of the principles are the same as Amazon. They too are insanely good at leveraging personalized offers and recommendations by using customer data through their mobile app and email marketing. They also have made buying easy. The Starbucks mobile app allows customers to order and pay for their order ahead of time, allowing them to skip the line and reduce wait times. Making the order process for your customers convenient and easier than your competitors will encourage customers to visit you more – and millions of Starbucks customers do just that.

Starbucks also uses urgency and scarcity with limited-time offers and seasonal promotions. They have seasonal beverages, themed merchandise, and their food items will "sell out." Promotions create excitement and encourage customers to visit more often to try new seasonal offerings.

Another area where Starbucks shines is their loyalty program. They incentivize customers to make repeat purchases by offering rewards points that can be redeemed for free food, drinks, or add-ons. And let's not forget that Starbucks strategically locates its stores in high-traffic areas. Whether it's a shopping mall, an airport, or a busy office corridor in your city, they make a point to maximize accessibility for customers. Buying frequency is synonymous with buying *ease*.

I know you aren't Starbucks or Amazon, at least not yet (*wink, wink*). But you can leverage the same strategies they use and adapt them to fit your specific industry and target market.

How do you calculate buying frequency (aka purchase frequency)? Let's do a quick calculation to show an example. Divide the number of orders/transactions by the number of unique customers over a specific period. For this example, we'll use a 30-day period. Using the same coffee shop analogy, if we have 1,000 orders and 250 unique customers over 30 days, the purchase frequency would be 4.

Calculating BF (Buying Frequency) / PF (Purchase Frequency):

Formula: PF = Total Number of Orders / Number of Unique Customers

Example: 1,000 / 250 unique customers = 4

That means each customer on average made four purchases over that one-month period.

Here are nine ways you can boost revenue and profitability through increasing buying frequency. The first three are strategies discussed earlier that also increase your AOV.

Loyalty programs: In addition to increasing your AOV, when implemented well, loyalty programs are a home run for increasing your buying frequency as well. Reward loyal customers for repeat purchases by offering points, discounts, or exclusive perks to incentivize them to return and make frequent purchases. If you have a physical space, consider rewarding in-store purchases with points or discounts, or offering exclusive in-store perks, such as VIP events and early access to sales.

Personalize the experience: Utilize customer data and technology to personalize offers and recommendations based on past purchases and preferences to increase your AOV and buying frequency. Implement email marketing campaigns, targeted promotions, and personalized product recommendations to encourage customers to make additional purchases.

Limited-time offers and promotions: This is also two-fold because it can increase AOV as well. Introduce limited-time offers, seasonal promotions, and exclusive deals to create excitement and urgency among customers. Use social media, email marketing, and other channels to promote offers and encourage customers to take advantage of them.

Subscription services: Offer a subscription service or membership options for products that customers regularly use or consume. Subscriptions and memberships provide a steady stream of revenue, increasing many metrics, including your buying frequency, monthly recurring revenue, and even your retention, driving down your overall customer acquisition cost.

Focus on convenience: Make it as easy as possible for customers to purchase from your business by optimizing the shopping experience both online and offline. Ensure that your website is user-friendly, has convenient payment options, and offers an easy sign-in process, and also consider strategic locations for physical storefronts or distribution centers.

Depending on the size of your business, consider creating a mobile app or online platform that allows customers to place orders and make payments conveniently. Consider offering a mobile ordering or mobile booking system to enhance the customer experience. It's a great way to make buying easier (and increase buying frequency.) Make it easy for your customers to get in touch with you. Have a properly staffed call center, email support, or live chat support to keep communication easy for your customers.

In-store events and workshops: If you have physical space, these are great ways to align your marketing budget and sales forecasts.

Even if you have an online business, this can be held in other physical locations.

Hosting in-store events, workshops, or classes related to your products or industry not only creates great marketing moments that drive customers' attention to one initiative and attract customers to your store, but also provides opportunities for additional purchases, customer engagement, loyalty, and increased purchasing.

Interactive demonstrations: Again, this is two-fold as it can also increase AOV. If you have a physical space, this is a great way for you to interact with your customers. Implementing interactive displays or product demonstrations in your store, hosting "meet the maker" demos, and sampling new products or services engages customers and encourages them to interact with what you offer, leading to increased interest and higher purchase frequency.

Analyze customer feedback: The fortune is in the data. Regularly collect and analyze customer feedback to understand their needs, preferences, and pain points. Have regular communication with your customers to understand their wants and needs. Use this information to continuously improve your products, services, and customer experience, ultimately driving repeat business and increasing buying frequency.

Exceptional customer service: This is more than two-fold, not just applying to your AOV and buying frequency. Customer service is the cornerstone to your business in many ways.

Ritz-Carlton is globally known for their customer culture and focus on customer experience. The secret to Ritz's unparalleled customer service lies in its strict adherence to its 100-year-old "Gold Standards." This culture is ingrained into everything they do.

Often when people are asked what company offers phenomenal customer experience, they say Apple. But when Steve Jobs was opening Apple stores in the early 2000s, he had Apple's future store managers attend the Ritz-Carlton hospitality training. Apple's worldwide success shows how borrowing practices from great companies, even those outside of your industry, can produce game-changing results.

If you make customer experience a priority, you make customer acquisition irrelevant.

Although it is one of the most valuable things you can do in your business, creating a company culture focused on customer service, isn't easy. However, this one focus will make all of the strategies to create *More Revenue NOW* that much easier.

This book isn't about customer service so I don't want to hijack the message; however, I like my books to be infused with knowledge that you can apply. Because ideas won't change your life; it's the implementation and execution of those ideas that will. So I'd be remiss if I left you hanging.

Creating a customer service standard for your business involves six key elements:

Define your philosophy: Clearly define your company's service philosophy and values. What do you want your brand to be known for in terms of customer service? For example, Ritz-Carlton emphasizes personalized service and attention to detail, while Zappos focuses on delivering happiness through outstanding customer experiences. How do you want your brand to feel?

Train your team: Provide team training on your company's service standards, policies, and procedures while focusing on topics such as communication skills, problem-solving techniques, and how to handle various customer situations. This is also a great opportunity to introduce role-playing exercises and real-life scenarios in the meeting. It's one thing to hear a concept; it's another to apply it. Reinforce deeper learning and create an environment that will encourage team members to practice and enhance their customer service skills.

Empower your employees: Equip your staff with the right tools to make critical decisions and encourage them to take action on resolving customer issues on the spot. Give them the autonomy and authority to make decisions that are in the best interest of the customer with clear processes and any guardrails needed. Encourage a culture where employees feel compelled to go above and beyond to exceed customer expectations.

Lead by example: The leadership in the organization sets the tone for exceptional customer service. Demonstrate the behaviors and attitudes you want to see in your team members. If you want them to respond with empathy, compassion, responsiveness, attention to detail, and commitment to customer satisfaction, model that for them and reward exceptional behaviors. Be accessible and approachable to your team members, and provide guidance and support as needed to help them succeed in delivering outstanding service.

Act on your feedback: Actively seek feedback from customers through surveys, reviews, and direct interactions. Use this feedback to identify areas for improvement and make necessary adjustments to your service standards and practices. By having standards in place to quickly respond to customer feedback and take concrete actions to address any issues or concerns raised by customers, you can solve any issue before it becomes a bigger one. Ignoring it or delaying a response can make the problem significantly worse.

Personalize your customer experience: Strive to personalize the customer experience whenever possible. Depending on the size of your organization, this can be handwritten cards, a personalized birthday gift, or knowing how they take their coffee. Take the time to learn your customers' preferences, needs, and pain points. Tailor your interactions, use their name whenever possible, and make personal recommendations accordingly. Use customer data and technology to customize communications, offers, and recommendations, making each customer feel valued, recognized, and appreciated.

Define Your Philosophy   Train Your Team   Empower Your Employees

CREATING A CUSTOMER SERVICE STANDARD

Lead by Example   Act on Feedback   Personalize the Experience

What value do you want to provide? How will you handle problems? What systems and processes can you put in place? How can you empower your team to handle problems as they happen?

The Customer Service Reflection worksheet can help you collect the answers to those questions and others. Spend as much time as you need to here because regardless of what business you're in, at the end of the day you're in the people business.

Creating Your Customer Service Standard

1 What is your core value proposition? How does your core value proposition reflect your company's customer service philosophy?

_____

_____

_____

2 How does your business uniquely solve your customers' problems or fulfill their needs better than your competitors?

_____

_____

_____

3 How can you empower your team to address and resolve customer issues promptly?

_____

_____

_____

4 What one method can you implement to personalize your customer service, making sure that your customers feel valued and/or understood?

_____

_____

_____

5 How can you systematically collect and incorporate customer feedback to improve your product or service offerings?

_____

_____

_____

6 Identify one system or process that can be created or optimized, to better serve your customers and foster a greater level of customer service:

_____

_____

_____

The bottom line is that every human wants to feel seen. Every customer has a story. Imagine if every customer walked through your doors (whether real or virtual) with a sign around their neck that said, "I am invisible to the world, please acknowledge me."

We just covered two foundational principles on how to grow your revenue. Increasing your average order value (AOV) through strategies like upselling, cross-selling, and loyalty programs will put you on the path to growing your revenue, as will increasing your purchase frequency (PF) through leveraging subscription services and limited-time offers (to name a few). We also broke down how you can make a customer acquisition strategy irrelevant by creating a customer service standard using six key elements.

But there is also a widely known yet often forgotten business principle that says this: success in business is determined by one thing – your ability to acquire new customers and _retain them_ for the long term. The principles in this chapter will set you up for success to do just that.

So let's get into it right now.

CHAPTER 5

Sniper Strategies for Viability

What got you to this level in business isn't going to get you to the next one.

"I just spent my last $25,000 to work with you,"

When Gary said that to me, my heart started racing. I thought to myself, I wish you would have told me first; I would have told you not to (no one wants that kind of pressure). But instead, I turned to face him. He appeared calm, collected, professionally put together, yet I could feel the concern and worry he carried in his body. He was dressed in an older-style suit with a white, not-so-crisp shirt and a gray tie. He looked like a nice man, middle aged, clean shaven, bald. You'd never know that he just walked up to a roulette table, placed every dime he had on black, and looked on as the dealer spun the ball around the wheel.

I hoped my face didn't reflect what my mind was thinking at that moment. Although it felt like 15 seconds went by before I uttered a word, I slightly tilted my head to the side, lifted the bottom of my chin in an attempt to lock eyes with him, and smiled. As I looked him straight in the eye, three words finally fell out of my mouth: "Let's do this."

At that moment, I felt like I was about to go to war with this guy I had never met before. And although we were only on a first-name basis, we were about to enter battle together. Lucky for Gary, one of the fundamental things that makes me, well, me, is my love of challenge – and when you're on tilt betting the last chips you have left on black – "challenge" is the understatement of the year.

The fact that this guy, whom I had never met before, had just wired my company the last money he had – the price of a small car, no less – well, it was game on. We were now *both* standing at that roulette wheel, together betting that ball landed on black.

Gary wasn't one of these guys who always dreamed of running his own business. He was an accidental entrepreneur. He had a doctorate and had spent a fortune on his education. He enjoyed his work, and his colleagues – but that all changed when Covid hit.

Obviously, the pandemic changed so much. Key industries were affected and some were proportionately hit the hardest – businesses like hotels, airlines, restaurants, retail, and manufacturing. Although the healthcare industry was in the bottom five of least impacted industries, alongside pharmaceuticals and communication technologies, in regard to market cap or job loss, the healthcare industry was crushed in a different way – with overwhelming demand, crippling supply shortages, and debilitating red tape weighed down by politics and bureaucracy. In the midst of it all, many healthcare employees lost autonomy and total control of their professional *and* personal lives.[1]

Gary was not all starry eyed; he was not prompted to start a business lured by the promise of wealth or power. Instead, he sought something far more precious – he wanted his time back. Years of grinding away, and then the added challenges Covid created, demanded more time and more energy, and meant Gary had lost his ability to have any normalcy in his schedule or any balance to his life.

One fall day, after months and months of working until exhaustion, living on fast food, Monster energy drinks, and espresso to keep going, Gary had just finished working a 12-hour shift. The head of the department walked up to him and said, "Sorry, bro, we need you to stay and pull another 24."

After working three 24-hour shifts already that week, Gary decided enough was enough. He had already missed every soccer game his twins had, his daughter's school play, his wife's birthday, their anniversary, and again missed watching the US Open with his dad on Father's Day, a tradition he and his brother started when their dad was first diagnosed with cancer when they were still in college.

That's when Gary reached his tipping point. And although it seemed abrupt to everyone at the hospital, and the department head was shocked when Gary turned in his resignation, this was something that had been brewing like a slow, hot pot of coffee for a really long time. Enough was enough.

Like Gary, I have had that feeling more times that I can count. And quite frankly, it's really served me a time or two or ten. Whether it's the employee you need to let go, the client you need to fire, or the relationship you need to end, often those moments of "enough is enough" is your conscious self finally acknowledging what your subconscious, your instinct, or your gut has been telling you all along.

For Gary, it was the final nudge he needed to take the leap and start his own business – a consulting firm specializing in healthcare. Like many new things, the first few months were a whirlwind of action-packed activities. There was a mix of excitement and uncertainty every day as he tried to navigate this new world. He poured his heart and soul into figuring this out, even succeeded at finding his first few clients, but as the months passed by, the accounts drew down and the bills piled up. That's when reality began to set in.

After a year in business, Gary found himself up and down and all around on the rollercoaster of entrepreneurship. As the exciting months passed by, he found himself right back in free fall. It was almost a year to the day since he left the corporate career, and he had worked so hard, only to realize he was down to his last $25,000, and no clients on the books.

He had invested everything he had into his venture, hoping that his hard work and determination would pay off. But despite giving it everything he knew, the clients stopped calling, and the prospect of failure weighed heavily on his shoulders.

That's when a friend reached out to Gary about going to a business event I was hosting. He immediately told his friend yes, and paid extra for the VIP ticket. Those who held VIP tickets had a scheduled meet-and-greet with me, Daymond John, and a few others. It was at that dinner when Gary came up to me and told me he had just become a client.

I saw something in Gary. Even though he had every reason to feel defeated, I could see the determination and could feel the resilience in his voice that told me he wasn't ready to give up; he just needed to be shown the way. I could also tell he was a rational, logical thinker who was ready to execute. I had a hunch that if this guy was able to commit to being in college for eight years to obtain a doctorate, figured out how to navigate having twins while in college, and found out his dad was battling cancer in the same year, then building a business was nothing in comparison.

You may think I'm talking in jest but I'm definitely not. I'm not downplaying how difficult building a scalable, sustainable, and sellable business is – just the opposite. It's hard, damn hard. But you've been through hard things before. You've overcome difficulty and challenge before. This might be of a different variety, but I'd bet that it's not as tough as some.

This is a key point that many entrepreneurs miss. Many underestimate their ability and miss the fact that what they've been through before are the very things that have prepared them for right now. You have been through hard things. There was a situation six months ago, six years ago, or 16 years ago that happened that you didn't think you were prepared for.

Having a baby is hard. Going through a divorce is hard. Suffering abuse and trauma is hard. Experiencing a health issue or receiving a diagnosis is hard. Moving across the country and not knowing anyone is hard. Losing a job and having to start over is hard. Losing a parent, a sibling, or a child – hard, hard, hard.

When you remember that you went through hard things before, and regardless of how difficult they were, you survived, you overcame, *you're still here*, it gives you hope, courage, and the belief that you can get through anything. Because you can.

That's what I look for in entrepreneurs – resolve. That's what you need to get from where you are to where you want to go. It isn't about having the background, a fancy degree, or an epicurean childhood. It's resolve and fortitude that separates the good from the great. You can have the best knowledge, the best mentors, the best strategies; but if you don't *also* have courage to continue, resilience to get back up, and belief in yourself, we will be swimming upstream together and may not make it.

I saw that Gary had all of this, even though he didn't see it in himself yet. My belief in him may have given him the courage to start, but his courage gave him the ability to continue.

We got to work. In our first session, I analyzed Gary's business from top to bottom, identifying strengths, weaknesses, and opportunities for growth. We developed a comprehensive plan that started with identifying his target market and leveraging digital and traditional marketing tactics, and then created a tailored customer acquisition strategy and personalized outreach to attract new clients.

It wasn't easy. He had some late nights and early mornings along the way. But Gary never lost sight of his *why* – the precious moments with family that drove him to start his business in the first place. And slowly but surely, his efforts began to pay off.

Within months, Gary started to see new clients calling, messaging, and emailing. He hired an assistant to help with the calls, and we set up a people plan to delegate, train, and offload other responsibilities on his plate. He stayed diligent and focused, and nine months in, he had over $250,000 in cash sitting in his bank account. His business began to thrive, and with each new level of success, his confidence grew. Before long, he was not only bringing in profit, but was just about to cross $1 million in gross revenue – a threshold that less than a year earlier he thought was impossible to achieve.

Looking back on those early days in business, Gary realized the importance of having a solid customer acquisition strategy from the start. Without understanding the science of customer acquisition or doing the work to build his own formula, he had been flying blind, hoping that passion and determination would be enough to carry him through. But with the right guidance, support, and a solid plan to follow, he was able to turn his business around *and* achieve the freedom he had once only dreamed.

Today, Gary's business is thriving, and he's happier and more fulfilled than ever before. It's been a joy to watch him continue to grow and thrive – having time for the twins, school plays, birthdays, and I know he hasn't missed a US Open on Father's Day yet.

The Science of Customer Acquisition

As Gary quickly realized, having a customer acquisition strategy is like having a formula for your business growth. It's a roadmap essential to navigate through growth, and paramount if you want to build a sustainable company that's scalable.

At its core, customer acquisition is about driving growth and ensuring the survival of your business. Just as businesses need a steady flow of customers to thrive, they must *actively* seek new customers to expand their reach and deepen their presence in the market.

Hoping people find your business isn't a strategy. Posting content on social media and hoping it results in sales isn't a strategy. Hoping someone tells someone else about your business isn't a strategy. Posting, hoping, wishing, praying are all good things, but combining them doesn't create a strategy destined for success.

Success in business is determined by one thing – your ability to acquire new customers and retain them.

We know that only 9% of businesses succeed, and those odds are worse than betting on black at the roulette wheel. Because if you want better odds than just letting it all ride on the green zero, we need to do everything we can to stack the odds in your favor. The most valuable chip you can have in your pocket is a solid customer acquisition strategy. In many ways, it is the central component of your business.

A successful strategy has a few core components: who, where, how, and what.

Who: A knowledgeable understanding of your customer – your target avatar, your buyer persona, or a detailed representation of your ideal customer. It would be the equivalent of creating a fictional character who embodies the traits, demographics, behaviors, and preferences of the people most likely to buy your products or services.

Where: A knowledgeable understanding of where your customers look for your products or services. Understanding where your customers are, both physically and digitally, is crucial for reaching more of them effectively. From using data and analytics tools to identify which marketing levers are driving the most engagement and conversions, to directly asking your existing customers how they found your business, all will help you uncover where your customers congregate. Monitor and analyze performance metrics while experimenting with different marketing channels to reach more of your target audience.

How: A knowledgeable understanding of how your business solves its problems or pain points. Identifying how your business solves problems starts with analyzing your product or service offerings. Evaluate the features and benefits of what you provide and consider how they address your customers' pain points. Look for ways your offerings can make their lives easier, save them time or money, or help them achieve their goals more effectively. By talking with your customers, doing research, and looking at success stories, you can gain a clear understanding of how your business solves your customers' problems. This insight is essential for developing effective marketing strategies and refining your offerings.

What: A knowledgeable understanding of what specific products or services solve that problem. Knowing which products and offerings solve your customers' problems or pain points is crucial for delivering value, driving overall satisfaction, creating retention, and increasing lifetime customer value. This can be found by conducting customer surveys or interviews to gather more detailed feedback on specific products or services. Ask them about their experience, what they like or dislike, and how you can improve to better address their needs. Test, reiterate, and make adjustments to ensure you continue to provide value and solve your customers' problems effectively.

A good customer acquisition strategy will lay the groundwork for long-term success and make your growth predictable and probable, stacking those odds further in your favor. It isn't about quick wins and short-term gains here. Your strategy is what creates the tracks for a reliable source of revenue to weather market fluctuations, or economic changes, more effectively. It's understanding the who, where, what, and how.

In a crowded marketplace, with everyone vying for attention and eyeballs, businesses *have* to stand out. The alternative is obscurity, which will lead to failure. I'm not trying to be all doom and gloom here, but a solid customer acquisition strategy will save you sleepless nights and a lot of confusion, and will provide clarity for you as the entrepreneur – simultaneously building awareness and reputation for the business.

By crafting messages that resonate with your target customer and by creating engaging experiences, the right strategy can capture the attention of potential customers and leave a lasting impression.

But perhaps most importantly, by analyzing data, and even your competitors, you can refine your approach, which will help you adapt to ever-changing market conditions.

In essence, your customer acquisition strategy is the foundation of your success in business. When done correctly, it will guide other business functions toward growth, resilience, and lasting stability.

Building Your Customer Acquisition Formula

Understanding the science behind customer acquisition – the who, where, how, and what – is the first part of your customer acquisition formula.

The second part is to assess and craft your unique value proposition (UVP). That is what sets your business apart from the noise and other competitors in your market, and communicates the value you offer customers. Your UVP serves as the beacon that guides all subsequent marketing efforts.

Starbucks is a great example of a value proposition in action. They didn't invent a technology or innovate something new. Starbucks took something that already existed and reimagined it.

Starbucks provided coffee drinkers with more than just coffee. They looked for gaps and opportunities where they could differentiate themselves and provide value in a way that their competitors weren't. Starbucks went beyond the caffeine fix and adopted storytelling and created compelling content for their target customer. They wove a narrative of community and belonging that resonates with their audience, evoking emotions and forging connection to their brand, their mission, and, subsequently, their product.

What Starbucks and many other titan companies have learned is that within the core of a customer acquisition formula lies a deep understanding of your target audience. By finding your unique value proposition, and effectively communicating the value you offer to your customers, you will differentiate your business and stand out in a crowded marketplace, which is essential for attracting and retaining customers.

Two great examples of unique value propositions can be found in Walmart and Nordstrom. The two retailers are both giants, yet their approaches to customer acquisition couldn't be more different because their defined target customers couldn't be more different.

To oversimplify, Walmart is known for its unbeatable prices. Walmart caters to the everyday shopper seeking affordability and convenience. Its target customers are families on a budget and individuals looking to get more for less. Walmart's customer acquisition strategy revolves around its core commitment to offer low prices across a wide array of products.

Through mass marketing efforts and a focus on convenience – with extensive store networks and seamless online shopping experiences – Walmart casts a wide net, drawing in value-conscious shoppers by the droves.

Completely on the other end of the spectrum lies Nordstrom, which – to oversimplify again – is known for luxury and exclusivity. Nordstrom's target customer is the affluent shopper who values quality, craftsmanship, and service.

Nordstrom caters to the individual seeking the finer things in life. Nordstrom's customer acquisition strategy hinges on providing an exceptional customer experience, both online and in-store.

They focus on personalized service from styling services to hassle-free returns, and go above and beyond to create an atmosphere of luxury and sophistication with exclusive events. Nordstrom cultivates exclusivity, unparalleled service, and access to coveted labels.

Despite their very different paths, both Walmart and Nordstrom have found immense success in their respective niches.

Walmart's scale and efficiency, coupled with its focus on affordability and accessibility, have solidified its position as a retail titan. Meanwhile, Nordstrom's dedication to luxury, exceptional service, and personalized attention has earned cultlike customer loyalty.

I think this paints a great picture of how understanding the unique needs and preferences of your target customers is key. That will shape your customer acquisition strategy and drive greater success. It *also* helps reverse engineer a stellar retention rate and improves all your other metrics. By defining your right target customer at the outset, you can acquire and therefore retain customers more effectively in the long term. More on that later.

Define Your Target, Craft Your Message, Choose Your Method

Before diving deeper into building the rest of your customer acquisition strategy, here are some questions to help you identify, or help you reevaluate, your target audience. Even if you've done this before, answering the following questions is an important exercise because the business landscape is always changing and your business is always evolving.

Target Audience Identifying + Evaluating

Answer the following questions.

Part 1: Define Your Target

1 What problem does your product or service solve?
What are its key features and benefits?

_____

_____

_____

2 What insights have you gained from evaluating market research, and what do you already know about your customers based on industry reports, competitor analysis, and your own customer surveys?

_____

_____

_____

3 What are the demographic characteristics of your potential customers? (age, gender, location, income level, education level, occupation)

_____

_____

_____

4 What are the psychographic attributes of your target audience?
(Interests, values, lifestyles, purchasing behaviors)

_____

_____

_____

5 If you start to look at and analyze your existing customer base, what common characteristics and trends do
you observe?

_____

_____

_____

6 What are the current pain points, challenges, and needs of your customer?
How does your product or service address these pain points?

_____

_____

_____

7 If you created a fictional representation of your ideal customer, including demographic and psychographic
details, as well as their goals, challenges, and preferences, what does your buyer persona look like?

_____

_____

_____

8 How can you test your understanding of your target audience? How can you validate these assumptions and gather feedback to verify these insights?

_____

_____

_____

Part 2: Craft Your Message

1 How does your product or service uniquely solve your customers' problems or improve their situation? Summarize this in a clear and concise statement.

_____

_____

_____

2 Given your target audience's characteristics, what tone and voice will resonate most effectively with them? Consider the balance between professionalism and friendliness, or authority and approachability.

_____

_____

_____

3 What is the single most compelling message about your product or service that you want your target audience to remember? Focus on the essence that encapsulates your value proposition.

_____

_____

_____

4 What specific action do you want your audience to take after engaging with your message? Make your CTA clear, direct, and motivating.

_____

_____

_____

5 How will you adapt your core message to fit different marketing channels (social media, email, website) while maintaining its fundamental essence?

_____

_____

_____

6 What methods will you use to test the effectiveness of your message with your target audience, and how will you refine it based on feedback?

_____

_____

_____

Part 3: Choose Your Marketing Method

1 Considering your target audience's preferences and behaviors, which marketing channels (social media, email, content marketing, traditional media, etc.) are most likely to reach them effectively? How do these channels align with your product or service's nature?

_____

_____

_____

2 What resources (budget, time, skills) do you currently have available to implement your marketing strategies? How does this influence your choice of marketing methods?

_____

_____

_____

3 What specific objectives do you aim to achieve with your marketing efforts (brand awareness, lead generation, sales)? How will you measure the success of your chosen marketing methods in achieving these goals?

_____

_____

_____

The key is to use this information to create or refine your customer acquisition strategy. This will inform your marketing strategies and tailor your messaging to better resonate with your target customer, taking them from awareness, to consideration, to purchase more quickly. That reduction in time and effort to convert a lead to a buyer can drastically reduce your CAC (customer acquisition cost) and make each transaction more profitable.

This small, simple act can help you stay focused on the goal behind the effort and will help you remain focused on the endgame, avoiding any of the entrepreneurial landmines we discussed in Chapter 2.

Having clear goals will not only enable you to align your effort and foster better communication with everyone on your team, but it will help ensure that the leadership within your business, and their teams, are working toward achieving the shared goal.

Convert Customers More Efficiently

Before you get more eyeballs on your business, let's make sure you have an end-to-end experience designed. Generally speaking, an end-to-end experience has three components: the customer's first point of contact with the business, the customer's interactions throughout their journey with the business, and where these two components occur.

I commonly see entrepreneurs skip this critical step and go straight for the PR tour. They think that "just getting more eyeballs" on their business will solve all their problems, but if you're not ready to capitalize on them and convert leads to sales, browsers to buyers, it can create more problems than you think.

Having a solid end-to-end experience will convert those new eyeballs into customers far more quickly, saving you time and capital. Not only does the approach help you acquire a new customer more quickly, with less money, but it also helps you retain those customers for the long term.

Here are a few highly effective strategies that can work for customer acquisition.

Landing Page or Website Conversion Optimization

Conversion optimization involves enhancing the percentage of sales or leads generated from your website traffic. By understanding your ideal customer profile in detail, you can tailor your content and offerings on specific landing pages. The personalization is found to create higher conversions. Even more important than personalization is page load speed. Potential customers will quickly bounce off your site if it takes too long to load or it's not responsive for mobile. With over 70% of website traffic coming from mobile devices, a responsive page and site that loads in under two seconds is key. Google has said that page speed is a factor in rankings and noted that slower load times deter users from engaging with your site. They said that two seconds is the threshold for e-commerce site acceptability, but Google aims for under a half-second.[2]

Fix any broken links or typos, ensuring all links on your website are functional and correct. Typos or errors degrade professionalism and diminish user trust. And make sure to check how your website appears and functions across various devices, test any and all forms for proper triggers, and confirm that any plug-ins are working appropriately. The goal is to ensure as seamless a user experience as possible for visitors.

Once these technical aspects are in order, you can begin testing and refining your conversion rate optimization (CRO) strategies. We've found that CRO is most successful when combining creative thinking with analytical approaches.

One of the most common is A/B testing. By experimenting with different elements such as headlines, call-to-action buttons, images, button color, and conversion paths (one-click checkout versus three-step checkout), you can start to identify which leads to higher conversion rates.

Omnipresence Marketing

Omnipresence (aka omnichannel marketing strategy) focuses on delivering a seamless and integrated experience for customers across multiple channels. While many businesses invest in multi-channel marketing, which targets individual channels separately, true omnichannel marketing revolves around the customer regardless of the channel they are using.

Whether it's through blog posts that educate, videos that inspire, or social media campaigns that engage, every piece of content serves to draw customers closer, taking them from brand awareness, to consideration, to purchase more quickly.

But a captivating story by itself isn't enough; it must be told through the right channels. The "right channels" in this instance are defined by where your defined target audience "hangs out." We can look to Netflix for this one.

Netflix creates exclusive content that captivates viewers. But that alone isn't the key to their success. By having seamless integration, an easy user experience, and an omnipresent content approach they have successfully used the reach of social media, the precision of email marketing, and leveraged influencer partnerships to expand their customer base.

Entrepreneurs must know where they are most likely to find their ideal client so they can strategically select the platforms that best amplify their message.

Testimonials, Referrals, and Recommendations

When I was coming out of "retirement" (in quotes because entrepreneurs never really retire), I wanted to build my next company's revenue and profit faster than I did in any prior endeavors. So I did a lot of work, interviewed and talked to people much smarter than me, and evaluated different approaches to see if there were strategies I could adopt from different industries to leverage for speed.

I reached out to connect to a colleague, the former CMO of Chipotle. I asked him how I could reverse engineer a marketing strategy to increase conversions more quickly. After talking through various things he did at Chipotle, he said, "You know what, Candy, I'd just add more testimonials. I know you have them, but I don't see enough of them." He started to spit out stats and data (which you know your girl *loves*).

On average, having even just three testimonials increases your chance of conversion by 32%. Imagine how much that will increase your profit, and decrease your CAC. So literally, if you don't implement anything else from this book, go add testimonials to every sales page and watch your metrics change.

According to Nielsen, approximately 84% of consumers trust opinions from a word-of-mouth source or a published review from other customers.[3] When you prominently showcase testimonials on your landing page, you boost your reputation and increase trust, and that will always win against a website that merely lists its benefits.

Social proof is key to earning the confidence of your audience.

Sharing experiences from satisfied customers allows you to highlight value without *you* having to say it yourself. This is particularly true for higher-priced products or services, where customers may be more cautious to buy.

It's vital to feature your most impressive testimonials and case studies. Put your best first. And if your business has collaborated with notable companies, highlighting them can enhance credibility.

Once you pair customer testimonials with tested calls to action, your browsers will convert buyers faster than ever before.

Here are four types of testimonials you can use:

Text: Simple text testimonials are the most popular and widely used testimonials on the internet. These are straightforward and to the point. They are additionally important because this is what Google utilizes for business pages. If you can, include a profile picture of the customer and, if applicable, add their title and company. You can even embed your Google reviews, which converts prospects similar to manually typed testimonials.

Video: Video testimonials can be a pain to get, but they can also set you apart from your competitors. Having your customer talk about your business, or how it has helped them, will speak volumes over text. Videos are more relatable, creating more trust, which can increase your chances of closing a potential customer. Consider offering a free product or service in exchange for a quick video testimonial.

Product review: I'll give it to you straight and to the point. Adding at least one to 10 reviews on your product pages will increase your conversion rate by at least 52%.[4] Amazon is a great example of this, as they have thousands of reviews for their top products. If your business is service based, you can still add reviews to your landing page and pricing pages.

Case studies: Having case studies is a great way to display your work to potential customers. You can turn the work you do, or have already done, into a case study. If your company has worked with big brands or big clients, these case studies should be visibly seen on the landing page to catch the prospect's attention.

And look, the data doesn't lie. I mean, just look at this stat. A whopping 89% of customers say they won't buy *anything* without checking reviews first. But get this – when they do read those reviews, it spikes the conversion rate by a solid 120%![5] Crazy, right?

Crazy or not, it's absolutely crucial to plaster those testimonials and reviews all over your website. Have them consistently throughout your site, and make sure placement is where everyone can see them. The big dogs in e-commerce have taught consumers to look for and trust those reviews. We can see in the numbers how not having them, when your customers are looking for them, can really hurt your conversions, your revenue, and ultimately your profit.

Success Leaves Clues

Just like Steve Jobs modeled the Ritz-Carlton, Warren Buffett modeled Benjamin Graham, and Elon Musk modeled Nikola Tesla, there is much to learn from studying the greats, regardless of whether or not they are in your direct industry.

Let's look at a few companies to identify what levers they've used to create their customer acquisition strategies that result in billions of dollars in annual revenue. The graphic shows key pillars of successful strategies used by some of the industry titans.

Company	Successful Strategies
amazon	• Personalized recommendations • Efficient delivery systems • Extensive product selection • Prime membership program
(Apple)	• Exceptional products • Focused on user experience • Word-of-mouth referrals • Hands-on customer support
NETFLIX	• Content creation • Personalized recommendations • Creates original content • Using data analytics to understand viewer preferences
TESLA	• Brand awareness through social media • Word-of-mouth marketing • Events such as product launches • Test drive experiences
Uber	• Seamless user experience • Referral programs • Offers promotional discounts • Targeted advertising to attract new users
airbnb	• Focuses on building trust with messaging • Attention to credibility through user reviews • Targeted marketing campaigns to both hosts and guests • Marketing focused on travel blogs and magazines

Source: **Amazon.com**, *Inc.; Apple Inc.; Netflix, Inc.; Tesla; Uber Technologies, Inc.; Airbnb, Inc.*

It's up to us as business owners to intricately design our approach to acquiring customers, but we don't have to do the heavy lifting alone. Entrepreneurs can draw inspiration and ideas from other successful corporations.

Because the reality is that you can have the most compelling content, blog articles, technology stack, and user experience and your business can fall flat without the right customer acquisition strategy. So to do anything, we have to start with the "one thing" first.

Company	Successful Strategies
HubSpot	• Content marketing and personalized email campaigns to entrepreneurs • Key sponsorships of podcasts and events • Offers free tools and resources to business owners • Created inbound marketing to convert more eyeballs to sales
JPMORGAN CHASE & CO.	• Personalized banking and digital experiences • Leverages data analytics to understand customer needs and preferences • Offers tailored products and services to different customer segments • Locations of banks also play a crucial role in ease and accessibility
AMERICAN EXPRESS	• Targeting affluent consumers and businesses • Partnerships with merchants and airlines • Offers unique perks, loyalty, and experiences to cardholders • Marketing efforts highlight the prestige and status
(Starbucks)	• Strategic location planning and coffeehouse design experience • Customer loyalty program with personalized offers • Utilizes mobile technology to enhance the ordering process • Social responsibility initiatives to strengthen loyalty
NIKE	• Targeted marketing campaigns and exclusive product releases • Brand awareness with major event sponsorships • Collaborations with celebrities and endorsements from top athletes • Personalized shopping experiences
ZARA	• Delivers the latest fashion trends at affordable prices • Maintains exclusivity and urgency with limited-edition collections • Rapid inventory turnover, frequent product launches • Omnichannel presence integrates shopping experiences

Source: HubSpot, Inc.; JPMorgan Chase & Co.; American Express; Starbucks Coffee Company; NIKE, INC.; ZARA.

A customer acquisition strategy is not just a nice-to-have for businesses; it's a fundamental component for your sustainable growth and ultimate success. By creating a systematic approach to attracting, converting, and retaining customers, your business can thrive and create sustainable, scalable sales, regardless of the next challenge lurking around the corner.

PART II

More Profit NOW

CHAPTER 6

Measuring What Matters

Only what gets measured has the potential to be improved.

"I think we're missing $32,000 from the month."

"What are you talking about?" I asked Jerry.

"I don't know, but something is off," he replied.

Jerry and I had our desks in the same office. Although we could have changed this arrangement at any time, we always kept things the way they were. We had a remarkable ability to tune each other out while we were working.

My cherry executive desk faced the door. Two black armchairs sat in front for guests. There was another cherry desk in my office that faced the wall, down to the left of the door – that was Jerry's.

I got up from my chair, walked over to his desk, and looked down at the financial reports he was looking at.

Jerry was an older man, in his early sixties, a former marine who had retired as CFO from another company one town over.

During a business lunch a few years prior, I was discussing that between expansion, real estate projects, and the nonprofit I started,

I needed to make some hires. I happened to share that I was looking for a controller, in-house accounting, a CFO – I really didn't know what I needed at that time, but knew I needed help. Delegating the financial aspect is huge, and it felt even bigger and more challenging to me at the time because that's the part I really enjoyed.

One of the guys at lunch turned to me and said, "I might know someone. He just retired but I'm not sure you'd want to work with him." The word "but" seemed to hang in the air for a moment too long.

"Might not want to work with him? Why not?" I asked. My question dripped with curiosity.

"I heard he and the CEO used to really get into it at times," he replied.

Since there was a lot to misinterpret with that statement, I wanted to clarify. "Get into it? Into what? Like arguments, and yelling?" I asked.

"Yeah, I guess he's former military and he has really strong opinions on how things should be done," he clarified.

I held back a huge smile as I replied, "Perfect. How can I get in touch with him?"

A former marine, from one of the greatest generations that existed, who focuses on facts, data, and numbers and tells you like it is? *Sign me up.* It wasn't a matter of *if* I could afford him; I knew it was a matter that I couldn't afford *not* to. I didn't care what number he needed; after one meeting, I knew he was truly a gift from God.

Jerry said he'd come out of retirement to "help me" part-time through a growth phase. "Maybe just a year to get things going, and then I'll hire someone to replace me," he said.

Well, that turned into us working together for 15 years. Jerry passed a few years ago. He was one of the best people I ever had the pleasure of working with. Our business relationship was cemented by the challenges and adversities of entrepreneurship that we faced together.

Although social media and the flashy smoke-and-mirrors marketing of today would like you to think otherwise, business success isn't measured by vanity metrics like followers, likes, or views. In fact, I have personally worked with those who have large YouTube accounts, millions of followers on TikTok, or a podcast with millions of downloads, yet they don't earn enough revenue, let alone profit, to quit their day job.

True success in business gets measured by a totally different set of numbers – like revenue, profit, and cash flow, to name a few.

In this chapter, I'll share a few myths and mistakes entrepreneurs make so that you can avoid them as fast as you avoid the shirtless guy and his rented jet photo on Instagram. Let's get into them.

Myth #1: Measure Everything!

Your business isn't one-dimensional. Getting an accurate picture of what's really going on means measuring multiple metrics and observing how they affect each other so you can understand exactly what is, and isn't, contributing to your success.

There are hundreds of different examples of key performance indicators, but there's no use in measuring all of them. Depending on your business goals, track the business metrics that really show how your business is doing. Tracking irrelevant KPIs will distract you from focusing on the things that truly matter. By doing so, you'll end up stressing about numbers that have no actual impact on your company's development. So it's highly important that you track KPIs; however, it's also highly important to choose the relevant ones.

A quick google search will provide an endless list of KPIs and metrics. As you read through the search results line by line, you may feel your heart pick up a beat – or 10 – until you become so overwhelmed that you go back to something else you were doing. This starts the entrepreneurial cycle of ignoring and avoiding.

I'm sure you've heard the common saying "Ignorance is bliss." But when it comes to your numbers, and ultimately your finances, ignorance isn't bliss. Ignorance is damn expensive.

It isn't a matter of *if* it creates problems down the road; it's a matter of *when* those problems will surface, not to mention how large they will be. Because even when you pay attention to your numbers, things can still happen. So just imagine what can happen when you don't.

But that doesn't mean that you have to track every single KPI and metric that exists. Unless you're over $25 million in gross revenue, it will be difficult to track everything. But if you're under that benchmark, you can gain a lot of clarity, and grow your profit, just by focusing on a handful.

In the sea of endless metrics and KPIs, how do you know which ones truly matter? How do you navigate the vastness of the financial metric ocean without needing massive amounts of diving equipment to understand them all?

There is a distinct science to building a business, a key formula that will steer your business toward profitability and sustainability – much like how Issac Newton used math and science to formulate the laws of motion and gravitation. We don't need to understand laws of physics to start, scale, or exit a business (thank goodness for that!), but when we use math and science to architect a business, it becomes far more probable that your entity will be profitable, scalable, and sustainable for the long term.

However, business isn't just science and math; art also comes into play. Part of the art is about knowing *when* to measure *what*, and how it relates to where you are in your build.

So what exactly should you be measuring? The answer depends on the nature of your business and your strategic objectives. However, there are certain universal metrics that most businesses can track to ensure financial health and performance.

The Big 10

I want to cover the Big 10. Yes, that's also the name of a college athletic conference, but that's not this. These Big 10 are pretty universal to most businesses, so let's break them down. We already covered two of the metrics in Chapter 4 when we talked about average order value and purchase/buying frequency, so here are eight more.

Just remember, only measure what's relevant to your business and its goals.

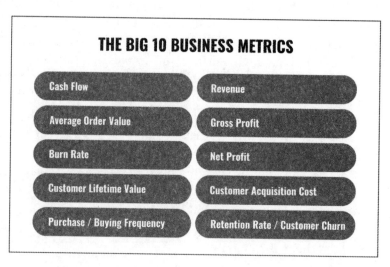

THE BIG 10 BUSINESS METRICS

- Cash Flow
- Revenue
- Average Order Value
- Gross Profit
- Burn Rate
- Net Profit
- Customer Lifetime Value
- Customer Acquisition Cost
- Purchase / Buying Frequency
- Retention Rate / Customer Churn

1. Revenue

Tracking sales revenue helps you measure your financial performance. It's calculated sales you make by selling your products, taking away the cost of returned items and undeliverables. Month-over-month or year-over-year sales results tell you how many customers are purchasing your products, if your marketing efforts are paying off, and your business's performance versus your competitors in your industry.

The information can indicate whether you need to make changes. However, it's good practice to not look at sales revenue in isolation when making business decisions. Instead, combine it with other sources of statistical information such as profit, customer acquisition cost, and retention (to name a few) to understand the bigger picture.

Sales revenue represents the total income generated from sales of goods or services and is a fundamental indicator of business growth and viability. Tracking revenue as a whole allows you to gauge the effectiveness of your sales and marketing efforts and identify trends in customer demand.

While revenue is important, it is **profit** that sustains a business. So next, let's look at two profit metrics – gross profit and net profit, which often get confused.

2. Gross Profit

Generally speaking, this is a very important and widely overlooked metric. Gross profit is the revenue generated minus the cost of goods sold (COGS). Variable costs are things like raw materials, production supplies, freight or delivery costs, or even packaging materials and merchant fees. Fixed costs are generally not included in COGS. Fixed costs are expenses like rent or lease payments, salaries, utilities and insurance, license fees, or loan payments – these are paid regardless of how much revenue you bring in and remain constant regardless of your production or sales.

Let's use the ABC Law Firm as an example. Legal services are the "goods" offered by the firm. Fixed costs such as rent, salaries of administrative staff, insurance premiums, and utilities are incurred to support the overall operation of the law firm but they are not typically considered part of COGS because they are not directly tied to providing legal services.

The firm's variable costs, on the other hand, may be included in COGS if they are directly related to providing legal services and fluctuate with the volume of work. For example, court filing fees, litigation costs, and travel expenses for court appearances are variable costs that could be part of COGS.

Formula: Gross Profit = Revenue – Cost of Goods Sold

Suppose the law firm generates $500,000 in revenue from legal services in a year. The total cost associated with providing those legal services – the variable costs, including lawyer salaries, office expenses, and so on – amounts to $300,000. Thus the gross profit for the law firm would be $500,000 – $300,000 = $200,000.

3. Net Profit

This one's pretty straightforward: revenue minus all expenses, including interest, depreciation, and taxes. It's the famous "bottom line."

Net profit is the revenue generated by a business minus all expenses, including both direct costs (COGS) and indirect costs (operating expenses, taxes, interest, etc.).

Net profit margin is your net profit as a percentage of your sales. Typical margins vary widely between businesses and industries, so make sure you're comparing properly when evaluating against industry averages.

Formula: Net Profit = Revenue – Total Expenses

Using the example of ABC Law Firm again, net profit would include not only the direct costs (COGS) associated with providing legal services but also overhead expenses like administrative salaries, marketing costs, utilities, and taxes.

Suppose the law firm has additional expenses totaling $100,000 for administrative salaries, marketing, utilities, and taxes.

In this case, the net profit would be $500,000 (revenue) – $300,000 (COGS) – $100,000 (other expenses) = $100,000.

Profit margins measure the percentage of revenue that translates into profit after accounting for expenses. By monitoring profit margins, you can assess the efficiency of your operations and pricing strategies and identify areas for cost optimization.

4. Customer Acquisition Cost (CAC)

This is a crucial metric to understand because it helps assess the effectiveness of your marketing and sales processes as they relate to revenue from new customers.

Acquiring new customers is vital for business growth, but it comes at a cost. By calculating CAC, you can evaluate the efficiency of your customer acquisition efforts and optimize your marketing budget for maximum ROI. A lower CAC indicates that a company is acquiring customers at a lower cost, which can lead to improved profitability and faster growth.

Formula: CAC = Total Marketing and Sales Expenses / Number of New Customers Acquired

Suppose the law firm spends $10,000 on marketing and sales efforts in a month and acquires 20 new clients during the same period. The customer acquisition cost (CAC) would be calculated as $10,000 (marketing and sales expense) / 20 new clients = $500 per new client.

In the context of our friend's law firm, marketing and sales expenses may include costs associated with advertising, website development, digital marketing campaigns, networking events, sponsorships, and inside or outside sales salaries during a specific period, such as a month or a quarter.

Number of new clients acquired refers to the total number of new clients that the law firm successfully engages during the same specific period, such as a month or a quarter.

Understanding the CAC is essential for all businesses as it evaluates the effectiveness of marketing resources, helps you identify which strategies are most cost-effective in acquiring new clients, and can provide insight into how to adjust your strategy to improve your profitability.

Analyzing the ROI on the resources you've invested in each of your marketing and sales efforts identifies what's working and what isn't.

5. Customer Lifetime Value (CLV)

Indicators of business success can be found in evaluating metrics like customer acquisition cost (CAC), customer lifetime value (CLV), churn rate, and gross margin as they serve valuable roles as it relates to the overall health and current growth trajectory of your business.

The metric is often denoted as CLV (customer lifetime value) or LCV (lifetime customer value), but the concept they represent remains the same.

It's essentially the predicted net profit (or gross revenue, depending on your method) attributed to the *entire* future relationship with a customer. While acquiring new customers is important, retaining existing ones is equally crucial. CLV quantifies the total value a customer contributes to your business over their entire relationship with you.

By understanding CLV, you can prioritize customer retention initiatives, enhance customer loyalty, and maximize long-term profitability of acquiring and retaining clients. It also allows you to focus on high-value clients and prioritize your efforts to enhance customer satisfaction and increase loyalty. This will help you make informed decisions regarding expense allocation, pricing, and how much to invest in marketing, and where.

The calculation of CLV can vary depending on the complexity of your business model and the data available. Different formulas may incorporate factors such as retention rate, discount rate, average purchase frequency, and average order value.

The formula to calculate can vary, so here is a simplified one:

$$\textbf{CLV} = \textbf{Average Revenue per Customer} \times \textbf{Average Customer Lifespan}$$

Alternatively, a more detailed formula may include considerations for factors such as retention rate, discount rate, and customer acquisition cost.

6. Burn Rate

This one is straight and to the point so we don't have to spend much time here. Burn rate is just as it sounds: how fast you're burning through cash. This refers to the rate at which your company is spending its available cash over a specific period, usually measured during monthly reporting. It indicates how quickly you are using your cash reserves before generating positive cash flow from operations.

Any business in the startup phase, or those undergoing rapid growth, will want to evaluate burn rate to monitor its cash runway and assess its overall sustainability.

Formula: Burn Rate = Total Cash Spent / Number of Months

7. Cash Flow

Imagine your business is the human body. Cash flow is the blood that keeps you alive. Without it, you're dead.

When you look at cash flow and profit, as well as each of their critical roles in your business, they are often interchanged but are not the same.

Cash flow is a crucial financial metric that measures the amount of money moving in and out of your business, and it is one of the best indicators of your business's financial health. It provides insights into a company's liquidity, operational efficiency, and financial health.

During your monthly State of the Union Meeting (which we break down in Chapter 7), your cash flow can be found on the cash flow statement, and your profit can be found on your profit-and-loss report (aka your income statement).

Cash flow management is essential for ensuring a business's ability to meet its short-term obligations, invest in growth opportunities, and weather any economic or market downturns.

Adequate, healthy cash flow allows you to know when to invest in your business – whether expanding operations, hiring new employees, or launching new products or services.

This is particularly crucial if your business has irregular revenue streams, high capital expenditures, or significant working capital requirements. If your business experiences seasonal fluctuations in revenue (such as retail or hospitality) or operates in a capital-intensive industry (like manufacturing or construction), it is crucial to monitor cash flow to navigate through periods of low sales. Accounting software such as QuickBooks, or business intelligence software such as Profit-NOW, offer solutions for better systems and cash flow forecasting.

Total cash flow represents the net change in a company's cash and cash equivalents over a specific period. It is calculated by summing operating, investing, and financing cash flows.

Formula: Net Cash Flow = Total Cash Inflows – Total Cash Outflows

You can learn more about my software company ProfitNOW and how we are helping entrepreneurs and business owners by going to **www.profitnow.io**.

8. Customer Churn and Retention Rate

While metrics like monthly revenue or sales figures are important for tracking immediate performance, it's also essential to consider long-term metrics that reflect sustainable growth and profitability, such as customer retention rates.

Customer churn is the number of customers who cancel your service or stop buying your products over a set period of time. This can also be known as customer attrition rate. In short, it is the percentage of customers or subscribers who stop using a product or service over a given period.

If you have a subscription-based business model, or leverage recurring revenue streams, such as software as a service (SaaS), companies commonly use churn rate to measure customer retention.

You can calculate your churn rate by taking the number of cancellations, or customers lost, over a specific period and dividing it by the total number of customers over the same period, and then multiplying that by 100.

Formula: Churn Rate
= (Customers Lost / Total Customers at Start of Period) × 100

For example, let's say you lost 100 out of 3,000 customers in one month. Your monthly churn rate would be 3.3% per month ((100 / 3000) × 100).

On the other side of the coin, we have customer retention and retention rate.

Retention rate is the opposite of churn rate as it measures the percentage of customers or subscribers retained over a specific period. Businesses with subscription-based models or recurring revenue streams can also use retention rate to assess customer loyalty and satisfaction, but retention rate is a metric that can (and most likely should) be measured by most businesses.

Formula: Retention Rate
   = ((Total Customers at Start of Period – Customers Lost)
      / Total Customers at Start of Period) × 100

Retention rate is calculated by subtracting the number of customers lost during a specific period from the total number of customers at the beginning of that period, dividing the result by the total number of customers at the beginning of the period, and then multiplying by 100 to express it as a percentage.

Reducing churn (and boosting retention) is crucial for business sustainability and survival.

On average, acquiring a new customer will cost you five times more than retaining an existing one.

Like I mentioned in the beginning of this section, there are an *endless* number of metrics and KPIs that you can use to measure the health of your business.

While some aspects of business success may be more challenging to quantify, such as brand reputation or employee satisfaction, there can be ways to measure these intangible assets indirectly. Depending on where you are in your build, implementing surveys, review mining, and employee satisfaction metrics can provide valuable insights into these additional areas.

Remember, these eight measurements plus the two covered in Chapter 4 are the Big 10 that apply to most businesses. The most relevant metrics for you can vary significantly depending on the nature of your business, your industry, and the stage of your current growth cycle. What works for one business may not be applicable to another. It's essential to understand them to develop your plan and tailor KPIs to your specific business goals.

Myth #2: Measure the Right Things and Business Will Grow!

I know I just told you that what you focus on grows, and that's true. But is that all you need to do?

Well, the single action of measuring the right things *will* improve your business, no doubt. But of course creating a profitable, sustainable business *can't* be that easy, or everyone would do it and far more than 9% of businesses would succeed.

While KPIs are valuable tools for monitoring performance and identifying areas for improvement, they don't guarantee success on their own. Effective execution, strategic decision-making, and adaptability are also critical in creating a successful and highly profitable business.

To truly harness the power of data and numbers, we need to do three things: set targets, establish budgets, and allocate expenses. By using these strategically, we can explode your growth and set up a path to scale.

1. **Set your targets.** Setting targets provides a clear benchmark for measuring progress and performance. Whether it's a revenue target, profit margin goal, or customer retention objective, targets give you something to strive for and help align your efforts toward a common purpose. Moreover, targets create accountability within your organization, motivating teams to work toward shared goals and objectives.

2. **Establish your budget.** But setting targets is only half the equation. Equally important is creating a budget that aligns with your strategic priorities and financial capabilities. A budget serves

as a financial roadmap, outlining anticipated revenues, expenses, and investments over a specific period. By carefully allocating resources based on your budget, you can ensure that every dollar is spent wisely and in support of your business objectives.

3. **Allocate your expenses.** Expense allocation is another critical aspect of financial management. Every dollar spent should contribute to the overall profitability and sustainability of your business. By categorizing expenses into essential and discretionary categories, you can prioritize investments that yield the highest return on investment while minimizing unnecessary costs.

I break this down further in Chapter 8 when we discuss how to implement the Expense Optimization Strategy.

Myth #3: Set It and Forget It!

I would love to tell you that you do this once and you're done. Man, wouldn't that be nice. Unfortunately, as soon as you nail your KPIs and measure what matters, you'll bust through a revenue benchmark in your business and need to identify a whole new set to monitor and create a different target and goal.

The myth that KPIs are set in stone is a fallacy that overlooks the dynamic nature of business growth and evolution. As your business continues to grow and evolve, your priorities, your strategies, *and* your challenges change. What may have been a relevant KPI during the startup phase may no longer hold the same significance as the company matures.

This evolution necessitates a continual reassessment and adaptation of KPIs to ensure they remain aligned with the growing organization's goals and objectives. For example, when you're in startup or early-stage mode, the focus is typically on growth – acquiring customers, expanding market reach, and establishing your place in the industry. Important KPIs such as customer acquisition cost (CAC), monthly recurring revenue (MRR), average order value (AOV), purchase frequency (PF), and customer lifetime value (CLV) would be paramount in measuring success and guiding your decision-making.

As you transition into a growth phase, the landscape changes. Business becomes more competitive, and your emphasis may shift from acquisition to retention – paying close attention to churn rate, customer retention rate, and even net promoter score (NPS) becomes your focus as these metrics evaluate performance and ensure long-term sustainability.

As your business matures further and enters a phase of scale, the KPIs must change once again. Revenue per employee (RPE), operational efficiency, operating cash flow (OCF), and return on investment (ROI) may be suited to better guide strategic decision-making.

Unless you have a trust fund or did a capital raise with no intention of giving your investors a return, you need profit to sustain through every level of growth – regardless of what metrics you are focusing on.

Remember, KPIs are not static. To be successful at every stage, they must be adapted, added onto, or changed to be aligned with you and your business goals. Failure to do so will put your business at risk of being blindsided by the ever-changing market.

Running Your Business with Intentionality and Focus

There is true power of measuring what matters, not just in tracking metrics or adhering to targets and budgets, but also in adopting a mindset of intentionality and focus. Running your business from a place of intention means making deliberate, data-driven decisions that align with your long-term vision and goals. It means constantly asking yourself, "Is this expenditure necessary? Does it contribute to our bottom line? Will it bring us closer to our objectives?"

Every decision, whether it's investing in marketing campaigns, optimizing operational processes, or expanding into new markets, should be guided by a clear understanding of the underlying metrics and their implications for your business.

By approaching business finance with intentionality and focus, you can create a more profitable and sustainable enterprise.

What if every business decision you made now you approached with one core intentionality and focus, and it's this: to eventually sell your business one day?

How differently would you think about your business, act on behalf of your business, move within your business, and decide where to place resources inside your business if you made decisions with that end in mind?

Even if that isn't your goal, the results you create by building your business with that intentionality will secure your place not just in the 9% of businesses that succeed, but in the top 2% of businesses that ever even have a chance to be acquired.

Which Metrics Are You Measuring This Quarter?

Measure What Matters

1 Identify one goal you are focusing on this quarter:

_____

_____

_____

2 Why is your goal important in general?

_____

_____

_____

3 Why is your goal especially important now (this quarter)?

_____

_____

_____

4 What will it cost you if you don't achieve it?

_____

_____

_____

5 **What will it bring you when you achieve it?**

_____

_____

_____

6 **Identify which metrics would measure performance of this goal:**

_____

_____

_____

7 **Re-write your goal in a way that incorporates these metrics:**

I will increase my _____

_____ from _____ to _____ by _____

Measuring what matters is not just about tracking numbers; it's about leveraging data to empower your decision-making so you can create a solid foundation for a business filled with profit and freedom.

You might build a business that you never want to exit, but how nice would it be to give yourself that option?

Intentionality and measuring what matters is a cornerstone in building a scalable, sustainable, and ultimately sellable business. By consistently reviewing and analyzing metrics that align with your goals, you can make your growth predictable, not just possible. To do exactly that, let's talk about holding your own State of the Union and get into the mechanics of how intentional efforts _with_ strategic alignment can create long-term success in any endeavor.

CHAPTER 7

State of the Union Meeting

No one will care about your bottom line more than you.

I had just stepped off stage from delivering a keynote. Jennifer, my assistant, had everything ready for us to transfer from backstage to the small room where I'd be signing books and meeting some of the audience for the next hour.

As we were walking through the hallway from the big conference room to the small meet-and-greet room, a woman in her mid-30s was walking straight toward us, waving. She had the prettiest red hair and her purple suit jacket made her green eyes pop. I could tell by the lanyard around her neck that she was attending the conference where I had just spoken.

"I did it!" she yelled toward us with a huge smile and both of her arms stretched out wide. Jennifer and I stopped in our tracks. I had no idea what she was referencing, but I knew she was very enthusiastic about doing whatever "it" was.

"Hi! What did you do?" I asked. She was coming toward us fast and closed the distance between us quickly. As she approached, I could tell she was excited, and beyond adorable, which put a huge smile on my face.

"I did the numbers thing you talked about today. I heard you talk about it on one of your podcast episodes and I did it!" she replied.

"Numbers thing – you mean the State of the Union?" I asked for clarification, because I talk about a lot of "numbers things."

"Yes!" she said excitedly. "I've been doing it for four months, every month, just like you said! My husband and I have a home services business," she continued. "After seven straight months of losing money, I found your podcast somehow and heard you talk about how to run the State of the Union. I never thought I was smart enough to help with the money part of the business. But after we lost so much money, I knew I needed to figure it out. And I did!"

My heart was smiling even bigger than my face. I learned more about Keelie's story as we stood in the hall and talked over the next 20 minutes.

The business she shared with her husband typically did pretty well. There was enough to make ends meet, support both of their salaries, pay all the staff and business-related expenses, plus have extra to invest every month.

So when the bank account suddenly seemed to take a hard right turn, and they had to start dipping into their savings to cover payroll, Keelie was rightfully scared and confused. After having to take $85,000 out of their savings over those seven months, she knew something was wrong. That's when, unbeknownst to me, our paths crossed. While waiting to meet a friend at her local coffee house on a Saturday morning, she was scrolling through social media and came across something about my podcast. Keelie decided to check it out, and heard me talk about the importance of holding a State of the Union for your business.

Her husband was away golfing that weekend, so she went into the office immediately and started to pull the financial reports I described on the show. She left the office, armed with more paperwork and documents than she had ever seen before, and grabbed a booth at First Watch, a breakfast-focused restaurant located in her town.

She sat in the booth alone looking over the reports. She said it felt like reading Spanish for the first time in high school. The first hour felt confusing and she was frustrated, but she remembered that on the podcast episode, "you told us to stick with it," so she did. One hour turned into four hours, but she found what was wrong. "Our best employee was stealing."

Although aspects were unique for her, her story has similarities to so many other stories from entrepreneurs just like her. In my experience, entrepreneurs love to learn about, or talk about, sales and marketing. They love to go to networking events and find ways to meet new people, but when it comes to their financials, numbers, and math formulas, they avoid it like the plague.

Yet, as Keelie had learned, it's the core function of business. And those numbers are telling you a story – you just have to learn the language.

How Numbers Talk to You

Beyond the science of business growth, the root of business finance is of course numbers and math. You may hear professionals use all kinds of fancy terms and financial jargon, but that doesn't make it more complicated – even though they may try to.

Business metrics and KPIs are the data.
Accounting is making sure the data is accurate.
Financial reports are just a summary of the data.
Financial analysis is how you look at the data.
Financial ratios are how you measure the data.
Revenue is the money that comes in.
Expenses are the money that goes out.
Profit is the money you keep.

The more money (revenue) that comes in and less money (expenses) that goes out, the more money you get to keep (profit). And in business, it isn't about the money you bring in, it's about the money you get to keep. Everything else builds from there.

Congrats! Now you understand business finance. I'm not trying to be flippant but you are smarter and more capable than you think. I see a lot of entrepreneurs stress over this. And I want to simplify it for you because all the financial people often make it sound so complex. Although what I'm about to go into can make many entrepreneurs' eyes start to glaze over, it doesn't have to be a snooze fest.

It's human nature to ignore things we don't understand, topics we don't enjoy, or tasks that give us anxiety. So if you've avoided your finances, there's nothing wrong with you; you're just choosing other things you are more comfortable with. But I genuinely want to help you become fluent in finance. First, because I know you can, and second because I know how much it will help you and your business.

Let's break down what to review to deepen your understanding and further develop your financial acumen.

Financial Reports Are Just a Summary of the Data

To have an accurate financial picture of how your business is performing, you want to use financial reports to review the data and understand the language in which numbers communicate.

This process helps you make informed decisions that have the potential to make a big impact on your business, your growth, and your bottom line. It helps you know what's working, if you're spending too much in one area, where you can cut expenses, and where to reallocate resources.

Because building a successful business, one with the ability to become part of the 9%, is at its core a bunch of numbers. Those numbers are telling you a story. If you want to create a sustainable, scalable business – or even build wealth – you need to read and interpret the story, just like Keelie.

Let's review a few of the biggest financial reports that you can start with.

Financial Report 1: Income Statement (P&L)

An income statement is one of three important financial statements used to summarize the business's financial performance over a specific period of time. It is also known as the profit-and-loss statement (P&L) or the statement of revenue and expense.

The income statement primarily focuses on the company's revenues and expenses during a particular period. It provides valuable insights into a company's operations, its efficiency, and any underperforming sectors, and can even give insights to its performance relative to industry peers and is very helpful. Your P&L gives you the ability to view the business's profitability, and empowers you to make informed decisions to improve the financial health of the business in the weeks, months, or quarters to come.

Remember that while they are very helpful, they can be misleading, too. If you have a large expense go out in one month yet sales revenue has remained stable, you may have negative cash flow on the report.

On the other hand, if you are a home builder and just contracted a new build, your income statement may show a massive influx of revenue and reflect positive cash flow, but those funds are in escrow for future expenses.

This is why I talk about the accrual accounting method in Chapter 9. Depending on the type of business you have, working with your accountant to determine if it's the best method for you may prove to be massively valuable. The more accurate your financial statements are, the more informed decisions you'll be able to make to grow and scale your business.

The graphic is an example of a very simplified income statement. The income statement for your business may be more complex, containing more lines or items.

Your Corporation

Income Statement
For the year ended December 31, 2024

	Total
Income	3,000,000
Service Income	
Total Income	$ 3,000,000
Cost of Goods Sold	
Cost of Goods Sold	600,000
Cost of Labor	750,000
Total Cost of Goods Sold	$ 1,350,000
Gross Profit	$1,650,000
Expenses	
Advertising	150,000
Bank Charges	15,000
Office Expenses	90,000
Travel	60,000
Utilities	30,000
Total Expenses	$ 345,000
Net Operating Income	$ 1,305,000
Other Expenses	
Depreciation	30,000
Total Other Expenses	$ 30,000
Net Other Income	$ 1,275,000
Net Income	$ 1,275,000

Financial Report 2: Cash Flow Statement

A cash flow statement is a great financial document because it's so dang straightforward. It's simply the amount of cash that flows in and out of the business. Unless there's fraud, cash is either in the bank or it's not.

Your Corporation

Statement of Cash Flows
For the year ended December 31, 2024

Cash flows from operating activities	$1,275,000
Net income	
Adjustments to reconcile net income to net cash	
provided by operating activities:	
Depreciation and amortization	30,000
Loss on sale of equipment	5,000
Changes in current assets and liabilities:	
Increase in accounts receivable	(-20,000)
Decrease in prepaid expenses	10,000
Decrease in accounts payable	(-15,000)
Net cash provided by operating activities	1,285,000
Cash flows from investing activities	
Capital expenditures	(-200,000)
Proceeds from sale of equipment	25,000
Net cash provided by financing activities	-175,000
Cash flows from financing activities	
Proceeds from issuing debt	150,000
Dividends paid	(-50,000)
Net cash provided by financing activities	100,000
Net increase in cash during the year	**1,210,000**
Cash at the beginning of the year	(100,000)
Cash at the end of the year	$1,310,000

A cash flow statement is a real-time statement tracking how much cash you have coming in and from where, minus the cash you're spending during a specific time period.

Cash inflow is the sum of all money that has come in from products or services you sell or have sold and are now paid for.

Cash outflow is the sum of any money you spent in your business on expenses, business activities, and investments.

Not maintaining healthy cash flow is the number-one reason that companies face bankruptcy and failure.

The cash flow statement is said to be the most intuitive of all the financial statements because it follows the cash made by the business in three main ways: through operations, investment, and financing. The sum of these three segments is called net cash flow.

Financial Report 3: Balance Sheet

A balance sheet is a quick snapshot of what the business owns, and what it owes. In a more traditional sense, it is a financial statement that reports your business's assets, liabilities, and owner's equity. This represents your business's net worth at the time the report was created.

$$\text{Assets} - \text{Liabilities} = \text{Owner's Equity}$$

Assets: what you own

Liabilities: what you owe

Owner's equity: what's left

The balance sheet is a valuable tool that can give great insight to the health of your business. This can determine solvency (if you'll have any issues paying the business's debts) and even reflect your business's "net worth" over time.

Just like the income statement (P&L), some assumptions may be misleading depending on the period of time you are reviewing. Your accountant or bookkeeper can help identify any assumptions or estimates that can interject bias in the numbers.

Your Corporation

Balance Sheet
December 31, 2024

ASSETS		LIABILITIES	
Current assets		**Current liabilities**	
Cash and cash equivalents	1,310,000	Short-term loans payable	50,000
Short-term investments	50,000	Current portion of long-term debt	40,000
Accounts receivable - net	120,000	Accounts payable	50,000
Other receivables	30,000	Accrued compensation and benefits	60,000
Inventory	80,000	Income taxes payable	5,000
Supplies	10,000	Other accrued liabilities	25,000
Prepaid expenses	30,000	Deferred revenues	30,000
Total Current assets	1,630,000	**Total Current liabilities**	260,000
Investments	200,000	**Long-term liabilities**	
		Notes payable	100,000
Property, plant & equipment - net		Bonds payable	150,000
Land	100,000	Deferred income taxes	20,000
Land improvements	20,000	**Total long-term liabilities**	270,000
Buildings	200,000		
Equipment	400,000	Other assets	
Less: accumulated depreciation	(60,000)		
Property, plant & equipment - net	660,000	Commitments and contingencies (see notes)	
Intangible assets			
Goodwill	50,000	**STOCKHOLDERS EQUITY**	
Other intangible assets	20,000	Common stock	200,000
Total intangible assets	70,000	Retained earnings	2,075,000
		Accum other comprehensive income	10,000
Other assets		Less: Treasury stock	(50,000)
		Total stockholders' equity	2,235,000
Other assets		**Total liabilities & stockholders' equity**	$2,765,000

Financial Report 4: Statement of Shareholders' Equity

If you don't have shareholders, the statement of stockholders' equity is often just considered the owner's equity and is found on the balance sheet.

If you do have shareholders, the statement of shareholder's equity gives any investors, owners, or shareholders (also known as stockholders) a picture of how the business is doing. This shows the equity of the business and any new investments that shareholders or owners made to the company, subtracts all dividends paid out to investors, and shows the ending equity balance for the period you are reviewing. This details the changes within the equity sections of a balance sheet over a specific period of time.

Numerous financial terms can be included. Here are six of the common ones:

- Common stock: a share of ownership of a company
- Par value: face value for a share of common stock
- Treasury stock: stock repurchased by the company from its shareholders
- Dividends: funds paid out to investors or percentage of profits paid to shareholders
- Retained earnings: amount of money left over after investors/ shareholders are paid
- Share capital: money the company raised by issuing stock

Now, since most small businesses don't have investors or shareholders, I want to refocus on the critical three financial reports you need for your State of the Union Meeting: **income statement, cash flow statement, and balance sheet.**

If you have investors and shareholders, you'll review the statement of shareholder's equity as well.

Financial Analysis Is How You Look at the Data

Confusion can lead to stress, and numbers can be overwhelming. I'm not here to dismiss any of that reality. But I'm going to share with you a strategy that will help you master your finances and will be a rewarding process – and kinda fun.

Trust me, this was an uncomfortable path I had to walk down myself decades ago and I remember how nervous I felt about doing this.

However, what I am about to share with you is the exact process Keelie heard on my podcast that helped her uncover the theft that was going on in her business. It radically changed her business, as it did mine all those years ago. Countless others have found that it has had a significant impact not only on their business but also their personal wealth.

I'm passionate about this topic because I know it works – and it's actually pretty simple. Let's walk through it step by step right now.

The State of the Union Meeting

You may instantly think of a podium, teleprompters, and the presidential seal but I assure you this is much different (and far more fun).

There are four key steps to conducting your very own state of the union meeting:

1. Prepare (or have your bookkeeper prepare) the three critical business financial statements we just discussed: **income statement, cash flow statement, and balance sheet.**

   To start, you will have three sets of these financial statements. You can always build off of this but if you've never done this with consistency before, this is a great set to work from.

TIME	DOCUMENTS
MONTH-OVER-MONTH	INCOME STATEMENT / P&L DETAILED BALANCE SHEET CASH FLOW STATEMENT
QUARTER-OVER-QUARTER	INCOME STATEMENT / P&L DETAILED BALANCE SHEET CASH FLOW STATEMENT
YEAR-OVER-YEAR	INCOME STATEMENT / P&L DETAILED BALANCE SHEET CASH FLOW STATEMENT

   This will build your 3×3. As shown in the illustration, you'll have three sets of three.

(3) Financial Reports: Income Statement, Cash Flow Statement, Balance Sheet.

(3) Time Periods: Monthly, QTD Comparison, QTD Comparison

If this is your first time doing this, or if you're at the beginning of the year, you'll also want to review the year-over-year comparison.

Don't worry about all the paper, and don't worry about what to do with all of this yet. Just print them out.

2. Next, gather your monthly **business bank statements** – paper statements if you're like me, or just grab your laptop if you like the electronic version. But I recommend that you print them out, at least in the beginning, and then decide from there. I'll explain why in a second.

   You'll also want a copy of your **current bank reconciliations** for the same month. (For example, if today is November 8, you'll be preparing October 1–31.)

   Whatever month it currently is, you'll review the prior month. If you've never done this before, I still suggest you do it for the previous month, because being overwhelmed will not help you in the beginning of this process.

   With your bank reconciliations, if you or your bookkeeper don't do this already, take any credit card statements, bills, loan payments of any kind that correspond with that month's reconciliations as well. Paperclip any bills paid out of the business bank account to the reconciliation reports so you have everything together for that month. (There are digital ways to do this, too, but I'm pretty old school.)

3. Next, prepare your **business software reports**. Prepare appropriate point-of-sale (POS) and/or customer relationship management (CRM) reports (the system or software you use to process and keep track of sales). In addition, prepare any corresponding sales data, customer data, merchant data, marketing data, or employee data from software, programs, or SaaS products that you use.

   Prepare and print these for the same month and/or quarter that you prepared your financial reports for.

The goal is to gather any/all of the reports needed for you to review in order to get a full snapshot of your business. This may include your payroll reports, any employee reporting on revenue per employee, billable hours or efficiency, any contractor- or vendor-related information needed, as well as any reports that reflect your KPIs and business metrics.

4. Now, let's get to **the best part**. I know I should tell you that developing your financial acumen is the best part of this. But my favorite part of the whole thing is actually something altogether different.

   The last step is to set an appointment in your calendar for a minimum of two hours.

As silly as it may sound, this last step changed everything for me when I started doing this 20-plus years ago. And without it, I don't think that I, Keelie, or thousands of other entrepreneurs would have stuck to reviewing our financial reports because I think this time is equally as important as the first three steps and makes it all worthwhile.

For that two-hour (or more) period, go to a cafe, a restaurant, a resort, a park. Go to your favorite brunch spot, your favorite place to grab a glass of wine or bottle of beer, or head to the local coffee shop that makes your favorite almond milk latte – and take everything with you. The point is to change your environment. Get away from the daily distractions or normal scenes of your work.

Take your 3×3 financial reports. Take your business bank statements with your current bank reconciliations and all corresponding statements. Take any business software or business intelligence reports for the same period. Leave your office, your house if you work from home, or wherever you typically work from. Grab a pen, a notepad, your laptop, and a highlighter if you want to go pro. Take those reports and head to the spot you've chosen.

Put your phone on silent and flip it upside down, remove the notifications from your laptop if you need to use it, and take off that smartwatch.

Make this a **recurring two-hour appointment with yourself every single month**.

By holding a monthly meeting with yourself (and your bookkeeper, controller, or accountant if you have one as well), you are making this a priority – because it is.

These meetings will enable you to stay up to date on your business trends as well as alert you to any unexplained increases or decreases that may tip you off to a bigger issue, giving you the opportunity to dive deeper.

Review the data to start to understand the language. You don't wait to review it until you understand it. That would be like waiting to invest your first $1,000 until you become Warren Buffett. Or waiting to throw your first football until you're an all-star quarterback in the Super Bowl, like Tom Brady.

Warren Buffett didn't learn how to be a billion-dollar investor by waiting to invest; he accomplished it by investing. And Tom Brady didn't win seven Super Bowls by waiting to throw a ball; he did it through consistent focus and putting in the work.

The same is required of you. If you can't invest at least two hours a month learning business finance and increasing your financial acumen, you'll never be able to create a scalable, sustainable, and sellable venture. To become exceptional at football, investing, or business, doing the work and putting in the reps are required.

Look, I didn't know anything about finance when I first started out. But once I understood that developing my financial knowledge was the "one thing" that could change everything for me, I became obsessed with learning everything I could.

Remember, it's not just important to know the numbers; it's important to understand how they apply to your specific business, and how they apply to where you are in your build.

Financial Ratios Are How You Measure the Data

Now that we have what we need to report the data, let's take a look at how we measure the data and interpret what the numbers are telling us.

You do this using financial ratios, which are a way you can interpret the data in your business and are critical because they provide valuable insights into your financial health and overall performance. They can help you understand how well your business is generating profits and managing assets, or how it's handling its debts and obligations.

By taking time to understand and analyze these ratios, you can identify areas of strength and weakness, evaluate your performance against competitors, or even identify potential problems before they become significant challenges. Ultimately, financial ratios empower you to make informed decisions that drive success and growth for your business.

Remember that consistently measuring, tracking, and increasing your knowledge will not only increase your wealth, but it can reduce your risk for theft, embezzlement, and fraud.

There are endless ratios you can pay attention to. However, you can learn a lot by measuring just a few. Understanding how well your business is managing its assets, generating profits, and faring against competitors and industry standards, as well as how it's handling debts and obligations, are all great insights that are essential for making informed decisions about budgeting, planning, and resource allocation.

This shifts you from the reactive role of responding to every urgent, nonimportant task in your business to a proactive approach that allows you to address problems early on and take corrective action before they escalate into larger problems.

So I'm going to focus on four key types of ratios to understand and apply: liquidity, profitability, leverage, and efficiency. I've found that these four apply to most businesses and are the ones I've used throughout six of my own builds.

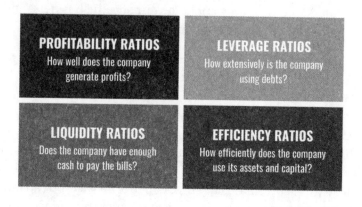

PROFITABILITY RATIOS
How well does the company generate profits?

LEVERAGE RATIOS
How extensively is the company using debts?

LIQUIDITY RATIOS
Does the company have enough cash to pay the bills?

EFFICIENCY RATIOS
How efficiently does the company use its assets and capital?

Profitability Ratio = Profit / Sales

Profitability ratios directly measure how efficiently your business is generating profits. They help you understand how effectively you're turning your sales into profits, which is essential for assessing your business's overall health and sustainability. This can help you identify areas where you may need to adjust pricing, control costs, or improve operational efficiency to maximize profits.

Liquidity Ratio = Assets / Liabilities

Liquidity ratios tell you if you have enough cash or assets that can be quickly converted into cash to cover your immediate expenses, like paying bills or suppliers. Good liquidity is crucial to avoid cash flow problems and ensure you have financial flexibility to handle unexpected expenses or downturns in business.

Leverage Ratio = Assets – Equity / Assets

Leverage ratios are important because they measure your financial risk. These ratios, like the debt-to-equity ratio or the interest coverage ratio, help you understand how much debt your business has relative to its equity and earnings. This is crucial for ensuring financial stability and minimizing the risk of failure or bankruptcy while equipping you to make informed decisions and maintain a healthy balance between debt and equity.

Efficiency Ratio = Expenses / Revenue

The numbers of efficiency ratios are endless. In the most general sense, the ratio measures your ability to use the assets your business owns and convert those assets to income. So at their core, efficiency ratios help make sure you're getting the most out of your resources.

I struggled with knowing how to best use this ratio in various businesses for years but once I was able to, it became one of the most important ratios because improving efficiency usually translates into increasing profitability. I'm going to summarize a few of them so you can pick at least one that may help you most.

Whether inventory turnover, accounts receivable turnover, or asset turnover, these ratios help you identify areas where your business can improve operational efficiency and optimize resource allocation. By improving efficiency, you can increase revenue, reduce costs, maximize profitability, spot inefficiencies, streamline processes, and make better data-driven decisions to improve overall business performance.

An efficiency ratio can mean something different to different businesses and different industries. For example, if you invoice customers and don't collect payment at time of the transaction, you can look at how long it takes to collect cash, or the time it takes for product inventory to convert to cash.

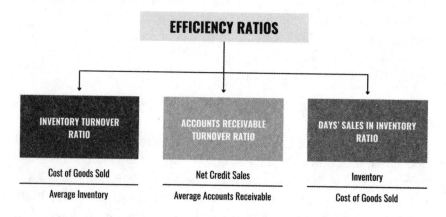

As I noted, there are endless financial ratios that you can look at and measure. When you have a business generating $25 million or more in annual revenue, you'll want to know several more than just profitability, liquidity, leverage, and efficiency ratios. But for most businesses, just measuring these four when evaluating your 3×3 financials will give you a great picture of the financial health of your business.

Important Business Metrics and KPIs

As you're sipping your favorite cup of joe, enjoying a slice of gluten-free coffee cake, or whatever your thing is – you need to look at a couple more things before concluding your monthly State of the Union.

In Chapter 6, we talked about how to measure what matters and broke down the Big 10 as they relate to some of the most common and widely evaluated KPIs and business metrics. By regularly monitoring these metrics during your SOTU, plus taking strategic actions based on that information, you can effectively work toward achieving your monthly, quarterly, or annual targets.

Depending on your goals, I recommend you pay attention to your gross revenue, variable costs, gross profit, and net profit as well as any business metrics that might give you insight to reduce costs and increase revenue – therefore creating more profit now.

Regardless of which metrics you identified in the prior chapter, there will likely be others that will give you a powerful advantage toward achieving your monthly, quarterly, and annual goals. Generally speaking, some others that may be valuable to you and your business are customer acquisition cost, average cart, average ticket, retention percentage, and revenue per employee, to name a few.

Now that you've compiled which metrics to measure, and you have all of your sales and financial reports for your SOTU, here is a word of caution. The worst thing any entrepreneur or high performer can do is try to jam financial reviews in between team meetings, customer interactions, sales calls, and creative work like filming all into the same day.

By holding your SOTU meeting in one chunk of dedicated time, as opposed to scattered all throughout the month, you can focus on the vitally important financial side of your business and not let it drain your productivity elsewhere.

Momentum Method

If you ever feel like a ping-pong ball being bounced around, you may want to consider adopting the Momentum Method. Batching your work, by focusing on similar tasks at once, minimizes the distractions of switching back and forth between tasks, thus overall maximizing efficiency. Use the Momentum Method by grouping similar activities together, such as responding to emails, making phone calls, or completing administrative tasks. This will allow you to streamline your workflow, reduce distractions, and make significant progress in a shorter amount of time, ultimately driving momentum and your business forward.

The Momentum Method is a productivity hack that saves you endless time, focus, and energy. This means that when you hold your

SOTU meeting, you may also want to set aside time that same day every month to update your personal financial statement (PFS) and review any investments you have. You're already in the numbers zone, so it's a great way to keep everything efficient and streamlined.

Depending on your type of industry and size of your business, during this time you may include updating your financial software, scanning receipts, reporting miles, filing receipts and paperwork, reviewing financial reports, A/P paying bills, A/R invoicing, collections, or hold a meeting and record minutes in your corporate book if you're required to do so.

It's always best to perform "like tasks" together and batch work to gain more momentum. It will save you time, money, and focus. So while you are holding your SOTU meeting, it could also be a great time to hold your shareholders' meeting and record meeting minutes in your corporate book (if you're required to keep them). This is an example of how you can batch work and stack habits.

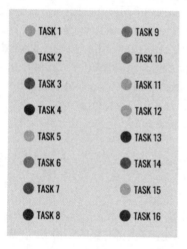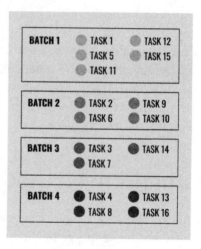

I talked about business structure in my book *Wealth Habits*, but it's worth repeating. Your business structure, and the state you live in, may require you to hold regular shareholders' meetings and keep meeting minutes. Make sure to talk to your business attorney to clarify your requirements. If you are ever sued or are part of a lawsuit, being compliant may save you time, money, and headache. You've worked so hard to build your business, it's important to make sure you're protected. I can't stress that enough.

My friend Cody is a business attorney and a pit bull litigator. He's the guy you want to protect you in court, not the guy you want to be against in court. He has successfully broken through LLCs and corporations on countless occasions and knows, unfortunately, it's not difficult to do in some cases.

Cody and I talked about a legal case in which the corporate veil was pierced successfully. The business owner (we'll call him Jack) had been in business for nearly 20 years. Jack's business agreed to provide services for a customer, a construction company (we'll call them ABC Construction).

After starting the project, ABC Construction alleged that Jack's business started the job but then abandoned the work midway. ABC Construction obtained a $400,000 judgment against Jack's business for breach of contract but was unable to collect on the judgment. ABC Construction then filed a new action seeking to pierce the veil of the corporation and recover the judgment personally from Jack, the owner.

Unfortunately, the courts can work around liability protection for various reasons: if the corporation is undercapitalized, if it doesn't maintain separate books, if there is evidence of fraud or illegal activity, or if the business's finances are not kept separate from the owner's finances and personal debts and bills are paid by the business. (I can't stress enough the importance of separate bank accounts and finances from your business.)

In Jack's case, the court went through and looked at each. There was no evidence that the business was undercapitalized; there was no evidence that the business was not a legitimate business – it was in operation for over 20 years. There was no fraud found as the business and its owner were both legit.

But there *was* evidence that showed Jack did not fully maintain a separate entity from his business. Although Jack kept a separate bank account for the business, he also commingled its funds with his personal finances. Jack used the accounts interchangeably for transactions, not just for this business, but for another business he had with his brother. Ugh.

The court said Jack did not adequately track the business's books, and didn't follow the required corporate formalities. He didn't have a record of his business's bylaws, corporate minutes, a shareholders' ledger, or documentation of a shareholders' meeting for the corporation.

Jack did file the required biennial reports for his business, but the reports were often filed after the deadline. This did not help his case and added weight to the other factors.

Therefore, the court ruled that the corporate veil should be pierced and allowed ABC Construction to recover the $400,000 judgment from Jack *personally*.

Never commingle business and personal expenses. It can be the quickest way to lose your liability protection. If this happens, like Jack, your personal assets (your house, car, personal savings) may be exposed to liability for the business.

It's critical not to have business transactions flowing through your personal accounts, and not to have personal transactions flowing through your business accounts.

Some of these things that I discuss may sound trivial or boring, but I promise you it's all from a place of love, protection, and support. It's easy to be distracted by all the hats you're wearing, and failure to pay attention to a few simple things can potentially have serious consequences.

The bottom line is this: the seemingly mundane stuff of owning a business – filing the required reports, holding the right meetings, and keeping proper books (shareholder, financial, and otherwise) accurate and up to date – are the very things that can prevent unforeseen problems. One of those unforeseen problems is your insurance policies. Remember to review your policies, make sure they grow as your business grows, and – depending on your net worth and the assets you have personally – please consider getting a personal liability umbrella policy to further protect you and your family. If you want to learn more, I discuss this topic in depth in my book *Wealth Habits*.

How Two Hours Pays Dividends

If you're like me, you've spent a boatload of time and money in unnecessary places thinking it would help your business but it just ended up hurting it. I don't want this to happen to you, and this State of the Union is the one thing I can give you that will help you trim costs, reallocate funds, and strategize how to build wealth within your business.

So I encourage you to take the time you need to invest in the skills necessary to build lasting wealth for both your business and personal finances. Who knows, maybe you start by doing the State of the Union for your business and it bleeds over into your personal finances, and before you know it you're balancing the budget with more wisdom both personally and professionally.

If you find financial information intimidating or fear your finances, you are not alone. The majority of the entrepreneurs I work with share that looking at their numbers is as enjoyable as going to the dentist. But after working together and developing their financial acumen, every single one of them shared powerful testimonies of how much their business improved and actually grew once this practice got put in motion. They ended up looking forward to their State of the Union because they saw how beneficial it was for both their business and their bottom line.

The only way to learn anything new is to start doing it. It takes time to develop excellence in your business, and this one practice will help you develop more confidence to make better data-driven decisions.

You deserve this for yourself. You deserve to become part of the 9% and knowing your numbers is the edge that helps you get there faster.

CHAPTER 8

Uncover the Profit You Already Have

You can't change what you don't measure, and you can't change what you avoid.

T ears welled up in Danielle's eyes. The words shook as they came out of her mouth, as if they were stuck in the back of her throat. The thought of saying them out loud seemed to make everything real for her.

"I have five months left before we run out of money."

As I stepped into the warehouse, Danielle and her husband, Paul, greeted me at the door. Their warmth and kindness was palpable. Our arms instantly stretched out and met for a hug and then a handshake. I could feel their distress.

For over a decade, Danielle's dedication to her business was incredible. What started as a fleeting thought she had in the middle of a cold winter night grew into a business generating over $1 million in revenue annually.

The business she started on a whim became successful enough to provide for the sweet family of five for quite some time. Fast forward to 2020, when the Covid-19 pandemic presented both opportunities and challenges for many businesses. Suddenly, her business saw unprecedented growth, nearly tripling its revenue.

But amid the frenzy of seemingly significant overnight success, Danielle made a critical misstep. Instead of consolidating her gains and reinforcing her business infrastructure, Danielle succumbed to the challenge of rapid expansion. She poured the increase of her top-line revenue into new websites and paid traffic that yielded little return, and hired a marketing agency that cost the business nearly $1 million within two tumultuous years.

To make a bad situation even worse, they were involved in a lawsuit and their financial reserves dwindled even more. Danielle resorted to desperate measures, tapping into funds from a real estate venture to keep the business afloat.

Yet, despite all of her hard work and efforts, the weight and the guilt of the problem hung heavy. It was then that Danielle reached out to me, seeking help in a last-ditch effort to save her business.

For Danielle, time was no longer a luxury. The urgency of the situation was underscored when I met her three beautiful kids. The gravity of the challenge and the task we had at hand hit me hard. I needed to create a strategic plan for a fast and decisive turnaround for Danielle's business.

The weight of the burden she carried was enormous. But one thing I knew for sure, this lady was a damn fighter. She felt lost, confused, embarrassed, guilty, shameful, and wasn't delusional about her situation – she *knew* she was on the brink of collapse, yet she *still* kept showing up and she was humble enough to ask for help.

When you go off to fight in battle, you want to go to war with a warrior, and I could tell that's exactly who Danielle was.

After reviewing her financials, gaining a clear understanding of her business, and taking a deep dive into all the reports I could get my hands on, I gave Danielle some immediate action steps to take and went back to my office to formulate her first 90-day plan.

As I drove back to my office, the words she said hung heavy on my heart: "I'm going to run out of money in five months." The fear and concern that clung to each of those words were palpable, but her willingness to roll up her sleeves and get to work was greater.

That's what makes a good entrepreneur great. Now it's time to get to work.

You Have to Dig Before You Build

To unlock the hidden profit potential in your business, it's essential to dig beneath the surface, identify areas of waste, and implement strategic financial systems to build a stable foundation for long-term success.

Although most entrepreneurs would prefer a hack, a scheme, a magic silver-bullet strategy that fixes everything right away, it just doesn't work that way. *I wish it did.*

In Danielle's case, she had negative cash flow. Her business lost money for 27 straight months. Before we could focus on *anything* else, we had to immediately stop the bleed.

The journey to sustainable growth demands that you pause and dig before you build (or continue to build). Each benchmark in revenue demands new attention on different aspects of the business, but all roads run through profit.

The reason for this is two-fold. First, focusing on sales in any situation without first focusing on profit (hemorrhaging profit in this case) is incorrect and disastrous. Second, focusing on increasing sales, sales, and more sales without having disciplined financial processes in place would be like trying to build a second story on your single-level house.

Regardless of whether your current slab is in good condition or is broken and falling apart, trying to add another level will create stress, cracks, and challenges that can result in bringing the entire structure to the ground. Similarly, when you have a business foundation built on inefficiency, dumping more sales on top of it will breed greater and more chaotic inefficiencies. Just as building another level on your house won't solve structural problems, more sales won't solve profit problems.

Think back on the challenging times in your business. Was there an employee you knew you had to let go? Did sales decrease but you ignored taking action, hoping it would simply get better? Or was the marketing company you contracted with not working out but you kept hanging on to it? The longer you delay addressing that firing, decrease in sales, or ineffective contractor, the more of your hard-earned profit you let slip away. What caused Danielle to get to this juncture in her business didn't happen overnight, and building it back wouldn't, either.

As much as you might hope for a "silver bullet" solution – a single remedy that promises to eliminate all challenges and catapult your business success – the reality paints quite a different picture.

Believe me, I would have *loved* a silver bullet or a white knight to come rescue me out of some of the jams I got myself into. But just as success isn't built overnight, that challenge likely didn't present itself overnight, either.

I call it the "slow fade" – a progressive decline, particularly in business. (I used the term for years, only to find out it's a dating term for when someone ends a relationship by gradually withdrawing from it. Who knew.)

The decline is not characterized by one distinct monumental decision that caused a challenge; instead the decline resulted from a combination of smaller decisions, or from ignoring and delaying decisions that in turn made the challenge become significant or grave.

Just as the slow fade of decline happens gradually, the process of rebuilding will take time as well. However, each step forward in the right direction can contribute to the cumulative momentum, propelling the business toward its goals.

Consistent, strategic forward actions compound and increase your business, just as compounding interest increases your money.

Digging down and uncovering what's under the surface is the first step toward growth (or stabilization in this case), and toward finding more money and more profit, now.

Trim the Fat on Your Expenses

Although being an entrepreneur can be exciting and exhilarating, the heart of this journey lies in the need for profitability.

Sure, we need to focus on finding customers, converting leads, and making sales, but one crucial aspect I see overlooked all the time is expense optimization. I love those words. Look, revenue generation is undoubtedly vital, but adding to your bottom line comes from increasing sales *and* decreasing expenses (or at least *maintaining* expenses while increasing sales). To have sustainable success, we need to manage expenses well.

Wisdom and experience has taught me that a more effective strategy lies in scrutinizing your expenses and identifying areas where you can trim the fat and make strategic cuts that will more efficiently translate to your bottom line.

Why focus on expense optimization? This math nerd is *so* glad you asked:

- **It immediately impacts your bottom line.** Unlike revenue generation and customer acquisition strategies, which may take time to materialize, expense optimization can deliver immediate results. By trimming the fat of unnecessary expenses, you directly enhance your bottom line, instantly boosting profitability.

- **It immediately provides more clarity.** Analyzing expenses prompts a closer examination of your business operations. This often leads to the identification of inefficiencies or redundancies that can be streamlined or eliminated altogether. Enhanced operational efficiency not only reduces costs but also improves overall business performance.

- **It immediately increases stability.** In today's quickly changing business landscape, financial stability is paramount. Identifying where you can cut or reduce expenses means you can optimize your build, thus creating a stronger financial foundation.

  Developing this discipline of focused expense reduction is invaluable, and will help further protect and manage cash flow, potentially even providing a buffer against unforeseen challenges.

But expense optimization isn't merely about cutting costs; it's about understanding what capital is going where and reallocating resources strategically when needed.

The Mechanics of Expense Optimization

When you reallocate funds from nonessential areas in your business and move them toward growth initiatives, you can fuel expansion and then look to new growth opportunities, like scaling marketing efforts or hiring top talent.

Cost allocations, expense controls, and budget optimization are all tools in your toolbox that help to lay the groundwork for sustainable growth.

Danielle ran this exact strategy and the results were astounding. Her efforts on the expense allocation saved her over $5,000 a month in expenses, resulting in over $60,000 a year. Maintaining average profit margins, she needed to generate over $500,000 in new sales revenue to result in the same amount to her bottom line.

Here is how you can implement the expense optimization strategy:

1. **Reduce nonessential expenses.** What expenses are truly essential and which are nonessential costs? While certain expenses are vital for day-to-day operations, others may not be. Perhaps at one time they were, but now they simply aren't needed. When you prioritize essential expenditures and eliminate nonessential ones, you can immediately reduce overhead and increase profitability.

2. **Renegotiate vendor contracts.** Take a proactive approach to your vendors and contracts by renegotiating contracts, shopping out competitive bids, and consolidating and combining suppliers to receive bulk or volume discounts. This can all result in significant cost savings without compromising quality.

   Look to negotiate favorable terms on pricing or payment structure on external service providers or independent contractors, such as janitorial, freelancers, or even marketing. For financial vendors and banking institutions, you can look to reduce rates or fees, regardless of whether it's a line of credit, checking account fees, or a reduction in merchant services fees. All can result in significant expense reduction.

   If you distribute or resell products, you may be able to negotiate terms related to pricing or marketing support or tiered discounts for certain volume requirements. Or if your business leases equipment, machinery, or tools, perhaps payment terms, maintenance, agreements, or warranty items could be up for renegotiation.

   This can even extend beyond your vendors or suppliers, which brings us to number three.

3. **Review overhead expenses.** Scrutinize overhead expenses such as utilities, office supplies, or rent if you lease. Whether it's exploring opportunities to downsize office or warehouse space, adopting a remote or hybrid work arrangement, or renegotiating lease agreements, this is another great area to consider when looking to trim the fat.

    Set up a time to renegotiate your business expenses like your internet supplier and cell phone carrier. Obtain and review new quotes for business, auto, property, worker's comp, and health insurance. And if you have physical locations, make sure you are on the correct electric plans for your usage, garbage collection, and shop rates for landscaping or snow removal.

    Even just a few hundred dollars here and there can add up to thousands over time. You should also consider energy-efficient measures to reduce utility costs over the long term.

4. **Reevaluate subscriptions and software charges.** This one gets me every time. When you have staff with expense accounts and credit cards, these expenses can rack up unintentionally and eat at your cash. It's so easy to overspend here, so pay close attention to cloud storage, website hosting, and cybersecurity. Expenses like Google Drive storage accounts, Dropbox, extra domain names, company emails, and hosting fees can really add up. If left unmonitored, other expense accounts like meals and entertainment expenses, SaaS subscriptions, business accounting and bookkeeping software, and POS or CRM systems can creep up and get out of control. Perhaps these are all services and software you need, but maybe it's worth exploring if there are alternative options that are less expensive and will still provide the components your business needs.

This practice is essential to minimize costs, streamline operations, and maximize profitability. Regularly reviewing and renegotiating contracts, seeking competitive bids, and maintaining communication with vendors can help you optimize and further grow your business.

The pursuit of sales and revenue is fundamental to entrepreneurial success; however, the key to sustainable profitability lies in expense management and optimization.

There is no one-size-fits-all formula for success, but your ability to trim the fat and optimize resources is not just something to hope for – it's imperative for survival.

Let Go of Bad Customers

In the words of Elsa, "Let it go, let it go-o-o. . . .I don't care. . .what they're going to say." In the Disney movie *Frozen,* Elsa had to learn and adopt the concept of letting go. Much rings true for entrepreneurs in the realm of business finance.

To create more profit now, you also have to "let go" now. Specifically, let go of anything that sucks the profit out of your business. If your business goes unchecked, it will become a revenue-eating enterprise. To create the wealth-generating machine you deserve, and have the edge to sustain success, assessing client profitability is one of the crucial steps to take on your journey toward sustainable growth.

Letting go of customers who suck the living entrepreneur – um, I mean profit – out of you is step one. I suggest you take a look at the 20% of customers who fit this category. (I explain why 20% in the next section.)

This one step achieves multiple things at the same time. First, it frees space to allow your business to serve other customers who don't drain the life, or profit, out of you. Second, while it increases your bandwidth to serve other customers, once you identify which customers are less profitable and drain more resources than others, it will increase your overall profit margins. Third, remember that customers may contribute to your top-line revenue, providing significant sales, but don't always correlate to significant profit.

When you see an increase in profit and a decrease in your overall stress, just imagine what you can accomplish. There aren't lines on our P&Ls with expenses like "constantly unhappy customer," "complainer who is never satisfied," "rude and aggravated customer," or "clients we break even on or lose money on but spend a lot on." So it takes some data review time to determine just how much of a drain they are on your profits.

I know it can be terrifying to drop clients, or a segment of customers, or even a whole vertical of products or services. I've done it more times than I can count in multiple businesses. At first it seems beyond scary, but after you have the data that support why this works, you too will realize this is a necessary step of business growth.

Identifying clients who contribute significantly to the bottom line helps you optimize your resource allocation and make better decisions when you look at profit, cash flow, and the overall impact on your financial health. And look, it's nothing personal; it's just math.

By freeing up cash tied to unprofitable or resource-draining clients, you can focus on acquiring and retaining more profitable ones. Doing this helps you become more efficient, further optimize profitability, and uncover money hiding in your business.

However, businesses often face the challenge of managing unprofitable clients. Despite investments in time and effort, some clients may not provide sufficient returns. Letting go of these clients is essential to protect profitability and ensure long-term viability. It requires clear communication and strategic decision-making, prioritizing the business's financial well-being over emotional attachments.

We covered the DEA strategy in Chapter 2, but there is a second D that I haven't shared with you yet that turns the DEA strategy into the DEAD strategy. That second D stands for duplicate.

> # You have to eliminate to expand

Once you identify what you can (D) delegate to your team, (E) eliminate the deadweight that's draining your resources, or discover what you can (A) automate to create a streamlined system or process, you want to look at what you can (D) duplicate to grow your profits faster.

Now that we let go of the *bottom* 20%, let's go get 20% more of your *best* customers.

Duplicate Your Top Customers

When you examine billion-dollar corporations, you'll find out that they are always looking at what efforts are generating the greatest results. The concept of "doing more with less" is another way to uncover the profit hiding in your business.

Large corporations and ultra-successful companies have no problem cutting products, clients, or services that aren't contributing to their bottom line because they know there is only so much "shelf space."

We see this same philosophy reflected in the Pareto Principle. Also referred to as the 80/20 rule, the Pareto Principle is named after Italian economist Vito Pareto, who observed that 80% of the land in Italy was owned by just 20% of the population. He realized that this pattern could also be found in many other areas of life, such as business economics and even personal finance.

Successful businesses are always looking to see what they can cut to maximize cash flow and profitability, resulting in doing more with less.

The Pareto Principle states that 80% of the effects come from 20% of the causes. In other words, 80% of your results come from 20% of your effort. This means that if you focus on the 20% that generates the most results, you can achieve a lot more with a lot less effort.

For example, Amazon used the 80/20 rule to optimize their product offerings and focus on the items that generate the most revenue. They also used this principle to prioritize their customer service efforts, focusing on the 20% of the customers who generate 80% of their revenue. Another example is Google, which used the rule to identify the 20% of their employees who generate 80% of their innovation and productivity.

Now, while the Pareto Principle suggests that we focus on the 20% that generates most of the results, we obviously shouldn't completely ignore the other 80%. There may be opportunities outside of that 20% that can generate significant results. So it's important to always stay open to them and be mindful of how we're spending our time, where we're putting our focus, and how we're spending our energy. But at the same time, we also want to evaluate those other opportunities carefully, making sure that they align with our overall goals and priorities.

The best way to use the 80/20 rule is as a guidepost, not a strict rule. Instead of focusing *exclusively* on that 20% that generates most of the results, aim to spend 80% of your time and energy on the 20% of those tasks. That means you're leaving yourself some room, some openness, to new opportunities that may arise.

This principle has been used successfully in the business world for decades. I've used this for the last 25 years and endless successful entrepreneurs have applied this to streamline their operations and achieve greater efficiency and profitability. So let's put it into practice right now and uncover some more profit that may be lurking in your business.

Finding Your BEST Customers

☐ Log into your POS, CRM, e-commerce platform, or software system where you keep sales and customer data.

☐ Review an annual report of customer data, including purchases, interactions, and demographics.

☐ Utilize your system's segmentation tools to categorize customers by their total spend, frequency of purchases, and level of engagement.

☐ Focus on the top segments and analyze them for common characteristics, such as demographics, purchasing behavior, product preferences, and how they engage with your business.

☐ Based on your findings, draft a profile of your ideal customer archetype. Include key attributes like age range, interests, purchasing habits, as well as preferred communication channels and what marketing channel you acquired them through.

Finding More BEST Customers

☐ Analyze the characteristics and behaviors of your identified customer archetype in detail, focusing on what makes them your best customers.

☐ Research where these customers spend their time online and offline. Look for forums, social media groups, websites, and physical locations they frequent.

☐ Identify the marketing channels (social media, email, direct mail, etc.) most effective at reaching this customer group based on their preferences and behaviors.

☐ Craft marketing messages that resonate with the values, needs, and interests of your customer archetype. Use language, imagery, and offers that speak directly to them.

☐ Use targeted advertising on platforms where your customers are most active. Apply demographic and psychographic filters to match your customer archetype.

☐ Partner with influencers or organizations that share a similar audience to your ideal customers to expand your reach.

☐ Encourage referrals from your current best customers, offering incentives for them to bring in others who are like them.

☐ Regularly review and adjust your marketing strategies based on the response and engagement from prospects to ensure you are effectively attracting more customers like your best ones.

When you think about your best customers, who comes to mind? When you think about which clients you'd love to have 1,000 more just like them, the ones who are just generally great people, the ones with whom you really enjoy working, and those who love you and your team and rave about your products or services – who comes to mind?

Regardless of your industry and what kind of customers you serve, if you were able to replace 20% of your worst-performing customers with 20% more of your best-performing customers, how much happier would you or your team be? How much more efficient would you be? How much better service could you provide? How much more profitable would you be? How clear would your marketing processes become?

But if just the mere thought of that isn't enough for you, let's gather some data. You'll want to look at things like how often customers buy from you, how much they spend each time, and how long they've been sticking around. If you have this data, look at any interactions they've had with your customer service team or any feedback or surveys they've given.

Once you gather that data, start crunching numbers. Depending on the KPIs you track, you may want to calculate things like the retention rate, overall profitability, and their lifetime customer value.

After you're done running those reports and evaluating all of those numbers, start to rank your customers. Determine who is doing the best in each category – retention, profitability, LCV, referral, and so on. If your CRM or POS system doesn't already offer this, look at how you could combine customer scores to get an overall picture of who your superstar VIP customers are.

If you have a loyalty program that tracks and handles this for your business, great. If you don't, gather this information and identify how you can keep them happy and maybe even attract more customers like them.

It's always good to know who your VIP customers are, how you can find more like them, and how to provide exceptional customer service so you keep them coming back for more.

Let's review:

1. **Collect your data.** Gather data on customer transactions, including purchase history, frequency of purchases, purchase amounts, and any other relevant metrics. Collect data on customer interactions, such as customer service inquiries, complaints, feedback, and so on. Obtain data on customer retention rates, including churn rates and average customer lifespan.

2. **Determine your data.** Determine which key metrics are important for you to evaluate customer performance. Here are a few ideas to get you started:

   - Total sales revenue: Total top line sales generated from each customer over a specific period

   - Retention rate: Percentage of customers who continue to do business with you over a specific period

   - Profitability: Revenue generated from each customer minus the cost of serving that customer (The cost associated with serving each customer would be any COGS, marketing, sales, and support costs.)

   - Lifetime customer value (LCV): The total revenue generated from a customer over their entire relationship with your business minus the total cost of acquiring and serving that customer

3. **Analyze your data.** Segment customers based on different criteria (e.g., purchase frequency, purchase amount, customer tenure). Calculate the retention rate, profitability, and LCV for each customer segment. Identify any anomalies that may indicate particularly high-performing or low-performing customers.

4. **Rank your customers.** Rank customers based on their performance in each metric you've identified as important to your business and industry (i.e., retention rate, profitability, LCV, etc.). Consider creating scores that take into account multiple metrics to identify overall top-performing customers and perhaps assign weights to different metrics based on their importance to your specific business goals.

5. **Systematize your data.** If you don't have software that provides this information for you, create customized reports that summarize the findings of your analysis. Present the top-performing customers in each category (i.e., retention, profitability, LCV). Develop a system or process on how to leverage this information to optimize your business. Consider taking the insights you gathered to create targeted marketing campaigns, loyalty programs, or personalized customer experiences.

Once you know *who* your best customers are based on the data, the next step is to determine *where* those customers originally came from so you can target marketing efforts to those same places and attract more customers just like them.

Create Your Blueprint

It's common for entrepreneurs like Danielle to focus solely on growing their business through increased sales and acquiring new customers, often overlooking how inefficient spending and poor financial management can erode profits as easily as a lack of revenue. Danielle experienced this as she had more customers and more sales than ever before, yet was mere months from bankruptcy. How does this happen?

It's like the insanity of trying to fill up a bucket with a gaping hole in the bottom; no matter how much water you pour in, you'll never fill it up if the leaks aren't identified and patched first. Understanding this principle is the first step. It does require that shift in mindset, from solely chasing top-line growth to adopting a better approach to business finance.

By being proactive on expense optimization, you can plug any leaks in that financial bucket and ensure that every additional dollar spent adds to your bottom line.

Effective financial management seems so boring to most entrepreneurs but if you can change the way you view numbers in your business and flip the script to realize it's *the one thing* that stands between you and your freedom – you'll turn into a heat-seeking missile charging toward your goals.

Managing your finances isn't just about cutting costs arbitrarily; it's about making strategic decisions that align with your business goals. Doing so involves analyzing your expenses, identifying areas of inefficiency or waste, and reallocating resources to maximize value. Maintaining profitability is striking a balance between investing in growth initiatives *and* controlling expenses.

Once you've identified areas of waste and inefficiency, the next step is to create a blueprint for financial stability and growth. But before we dive into how to create your blueprint, remember the pillar point I keep hammering home: boosting revenue isn't a clear path to profitability. Businesses lose so much money due to overspending and/or mismanagement of resources.

So how can you spot these profit leaks and plug them?

There are three not-so-sexy things you need to put in place if you don't already have them: **a budget, a financial forecast, and expense allocation.** By doing so, you can start to stack the odds in your favor to ensure long-term success.

But here's the thing: business finance is actually simple. The more money you make and the less you spend, the greater your ability to invest more money. This allows you to create a wealth-generating machine that practically prints money, so you don't have to constantly trade time for it. And if *that's* not sexy, I don't know what is.

Look, I'm not here to motivate you to do any of this. Motivation isn't going to change your business or your finances. Quite frankly, reading the *idea* of taking responsibility for your financial health isn't going to change your business, either.

What's going to change your business, and create a whole new level of growth, is the *implementation* and *execution* of the idea. That, and that alone, will result in a whole new level of growth – not just for your business, but for you as an entrepreneur.

Financial Budgeting

Developing a comprehensive budget is a fundamental aspect of financial management for any business and provides a roadmap for your financial performance. It helps in setting goals, allocating resources efficiently, managing risks, and making informed decisions. It also instills confidence in you, the entrepreneur (as well as any investors or stakeholders), because it enables businesses to monitor performance closely.

Without a budget, you run the risk of overextending resources and being unprepared for any market shifts or revenue downturns. Overall, it is essential for guiding data-driven decision-making and ensuring the long-term financial health of your business while mitigating risks and increasing sustainability.

Here are four steps to create a simple and streamlined budget.

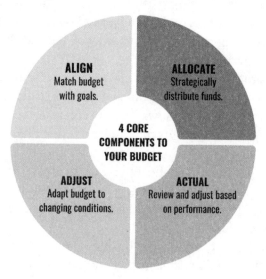

Align

Ensure that your budget aligns closely with your business goals and strategic priorities. Each budget line item should serve a specific purpose in advancing your overarching objectives.

Allocate

Allocate funds strategically across key areas of your business. For example, allocate a sufficient budget for marketing to attract new customers and promote brand awareness, allocate funds for operations to ensure smooth day-to-day functioning, allocate resources for research and development to foster innovation, and allocate funds for capital investments to support long-term growth and expansion.

Actual

Continuously monitor your actual performance against budgeted targets. This involves regularly reviewing financial reports, comparing actual expenses and revenues to budgeted amounts, and identifying any variances or discrepancies.

By monitoring performance in real time, you can quickly identify areas of concern and take corrective action as needed.

Adjust

Remain flexible and be prepared to adjust your budget as circumstances change. Business conditions are often fluid, and unexpected events or opportunities may arise that necessitate modifications to your budget. Regularly reassess your budget assumptions and make adjustments as needed to ensure that your financial resources are being allocated effectively.

In Danielle's business, her marketing efforts resulted in a significant increase in sales throughout Covid; however, because she wasn't aware of budgeting or the financial components of her business, her revenue – and ultimately her business – was driving itself with no real destination. Leaving any business to drive itself is disastrous.

Having a streamlined budget and a financial forecast puts you in the driver's seat of your business to strategically align it to your goals, adapt to changing conditions, and adjust to performance in real time.

Financial Forecasts

So here's the short of it. A financial forecast predicts how your business is going to perform financially over a certain period of time. It's like looking into a crystal ball (well, not quite that magical, but you get the idea) to see where your business is headed financially. Financial forecasting is a critical tool for anticipating future financial performance and making informed business decisions.

Now, why is it important? Well, imagine you're driving a car without knowing how to get to where you want to go. You might end up lost, right? In business, a financial forecast helps you avoid that feeling of being lost. It gives you a clear picture of what to expect financially, so you can make strategic data-driven decisions. That sense of clarity and resolve will be like adding rocket fuel to the fire of growth.

Just like you plan your route before a trip, a financial forecast helps you plan for the future of your business. You can anticipate expenses, predict cash flow, and set realistic financial goals, allowing you to make better decisions about things like investments, hiring, pricing, and new offers.

By looking at past data and projecting into the future, you can spot any cyclical revenue trends in your business. Maybe sales tend to dip during certain months, or you see a pattern in customer behavior. A forecast helps you prepare for these trends and create a plan to counterbalance them when necessary.

And if you ever need to borrow money, bring on investors, or even participate in a merger, having a solid financial forecast can provide confidence in your business. It displays that you've thought things through and have a plan for financial success.

Once you've developed your financial forecast, you can use it as a benchmark to track actual performance against. This helps you stay on course toward your business goals and helps you make quick adjustments if things aren't going as planned.

Financial Forecasting Resource

ANTICIPATED COLLECTIONS			Checking	
Anticipated Collections			Petty Cash	
PAYMENTS			Savings	
Accounts Payable			Beginning Cash Balance	
Credit Cards/LOC			Projected Cash Balance	
Personnel			Net Change in Cash	
Sales & Marketing				
Facilities & Equipment				
General & Administrative				
Taxes				
Loans				
Distributions				
CREDIT CARD BALANCES				
Credit Card 1			Credit Line	
Credit Card 2				

	CURRENT	PAST 30	PAST 60	PAST 90	PAST 120	TODAY
Receivables						
Payables						

How to develop your own financial forecast:

1. Analyze past performance metrics, such as sales revenue, expenses, and cash flow, to identify patterns and trends that can inform your forecasts. Utilize any of your own historical data, as well as any

market trends or industry benchmarks, to develop realistic financial projections.

2. Review this data to make strategic decisions on where to allocate your resources: where to invest in marketing initiatives, what areas need cost-saving measures in place, and create a cash flow forecast to plan for future capital expenditures, hiring talent, or debt repayments.

3. Regularly review and revise your assumptions, incorporate actual data as it becomes available, and adjust your forecasts accordingly to ensure accuracy and relevance. Refine your financial forecasts based on new information as it presents.

4. Assess the potential impact of different business scenarios on your financial projections, such as best-case, worst-case, and also the most likely scenarios, to evaluate the range of possible outcomes and any underlying risks.

In a nutshell, a financial forecast is like the GPS for your business. The bigger your business gets, and the more revenue you bring in, the more critical these become. It ultimately helps you navigate the twists and turns of ever-changing revenue and expenses, and is an important tool that helps keep you on the road to success.

Expense Allocations

Expense allocations is just a fancy finance term for pizza. They are basically a way of divvying up your business expenses to different categories or departments. Like splitting up a pizza among friends – each slice goes to someone or something – and we already know who is going to eat more than just one slice.

Now, why is this important? Well, expense allocations help you understand where your money is going and how it's being used in your business. Accurate expense allocation is essential for understanding the true cost of your products or services and optimizing your pricing strategies. By categorizing your expenses, you get a clearer picture of where your money is being spent. You can see how much you're spending on things like marketing, salaries, supplies, and so on. This clarity helps you make better decisions about where to allocate resources in the future.

This is also key for creating a budget. When you know how much you're spending in each category, you can set realistic budget targets for the future. This removes the classic entrepreneurial feeling of throwing things against the wall to see what sticks. It helps you manage your cash flow more effectively, and avoid any overspending.

Once you've allocated your expenses, you can analyze each category to see if there are any areas where you might be overspending or where you could cut costs. Having cost controls helps you optimize your expenses and improve your bottom line. As your business continues to grow, they can also be used to evaluate the performance of different departments or projects within your organization. By comparing actual expenses against budgeted expenses, you see how well each area is managing resources.

Spending an hour or two on this every month will give you 10 times the amount of clarity and confidence to make decisions in your business.

Now, I could get into activity-based costing (ABC) and how to use it, but for most businesses, it's complete overkill. For the biggest bang for your buck, you can use expense allocations in a very easy direct way: to identify opportunities to reduce cost and improve efficiency; to identify any products, services, offers, departments, or projects with high expense-to-revenue ratios; and find ways to streamline processes, reduce waste, or reallocate resources to more profitable ones.

Overall, expense allocations help you understand where you've been, where you're going, and how to get there in the most efficient way possible. When you understand what they are and how they can help, you just might like them. The next time you sit down to work on these, order a pizza and just have fun with it. I mean, isn't everything better with pizza?

Remember, growth and scale are not one and the same. Focusing on increasing your sales without first implementing the steps outlined in this chapter is dangerous because it will likely create more inefficiencies and greater expenses – further eroding your bottom line.

When you pause to optimize your costs, trim the fat on your expenses, let go of profit-draining customers, duplicate your top-performing customers, and create your financial blueprint with budgeting, forecasting, and allocations, you've created the perfect storm to uncover hidden profit in your business and increase overall profitability. Now who doesn't want that?

CHAPTER 9

The Players on Your Profit Team

"In both sports and business, you have to play to win. It's about strategy, execution, and never giving up."

— Alex Rodriguez

I had just walked out of a private venture capital meeting with a Middle Eastern prince, the owner of an MLB team, and an owner of an NBA team. Just as we stood up from the table to leave the meeting, Seth Gorgon and the Dalai Lama walked by.

You'd think I was setting up a joke with that opener, but that actually happened. There were owners of major media networks, celebrities, and billionaire tech founders at this meeting, among others.

The first few minutes I was thinking, how on earth am I sitting here? If they knew I grew up in a trailer with zero formal education, I'd surely be asked to leave. Yet there I sat – with a friend who is a champion athlete, investor and businessman with $800M assets under management.

After the meeting, everyone went back to a house in the hills of LA. The views from the back of the house went on for miles. The water from the infinity pool spilled over the edge and sent serene sounds into the air as the fire feature created the ambience of a sanctuary. As the large glass pocket door opened, the inside met with the outside, as did smells from the kitchen as a chef prepared a gorgeous dinner.

Again, the same thought that I had from our business meeting earlier in the day entered my mind as I looked out at the view one more time: *How on earth am I sitting here?*

The Game of Sports and Business

Full disclosure: I've never been into sports. My dad didn't watch any, I didn't have any brothers, and we were so poor that sports just weren't on our radar. Growing up, my parents and I always worked on the weekends so there weren't any Sunday games, trips to the ballpark, or Super Bowl traditions. I was in my mid-20s by the time I even watched my first full football game. Well, actually watching my first game turned into watching *games.*

A new guy asked me out on a date to grab lunch and "watch the game." I thought, how bad can that be? I'll have a drink, grab a salad, and "watch the game." I thought I was going on a one- or two-hour date. I couldn't believe how long one game took, and was horrified when I learned that there was more than just that one game on. Games at one o' clock, four o' clock, and seven o' clock – all in a row!

Unlike my thought after that business meeting, this time I was thinking, "How on earth can I get out of here!" I share that in order to share this: regardless of whether or not you like sports, there's a lot we can take from it and apply in the business world.

Mark Cuban, billionaire entrepreneur, Shark Tank investor, and owner of the Dallas Mavericks, said, "Success in business is the result of discipline, hard work, and perseverance, just like winning a game." He is a great example of understanding how business and sports both involve competition as he's heavily involved in both worlds at the highest level.

Whether it's competing for market share, customers, or victories – competitors are constantly striving to outperform each other and achieve their goals, and success is often measured by achieving specific goals. Whether it's winning a division championship, or hitting quarterly revenue targets, setting goals and measuring your progress toward them is not only fundamental, but it's required for the 9% edge.

Just as athletes and their coaches must collaborate effectively to win games, entrepreneurs and their employees must work together cohesively and empower others to be the best in their role. Both rely heavily on teamwork, strategic direction, and executing the correct strategy to navigate challenges, capitalize on opportunities, and achieve long-term success.

How can you adopt the fundamental principles used throughout sports and adapt them to business? How can you identify which players you need to recruit to create your championship team?

Just as in sports, having the right people in the right positions on your financial team is pivotal for the edge. Let's talk about whom to draft for the players on your very own Profit Team.

Creating Your Championship Team

Magic Johnson achieved what only three other athletes ever have accomplished: he became a billionaire, joining Michael Jordan, Tiger Woods, and Lebron James. Magic is a widely recognized athlete who is well known both on and off the court.

In addition to having stakes in MLB, NFL, and WNBA teams, he made a historic investment, obtaining control of Pepsi, owned over 100 Starbucks locations, has equity in the insurance and financial services industry, and has owned businesses ranging from Burger Kings to health clubs. When asked what led to this enormous success, he said, "Success on the court and in business is all about teamwork, leadership, and a relentless drive to win."

One of the smartest things that athletes and sports teams do is that they specialize in their positions. The quarterback doesn't moonlight as the punter. The offensive lineman isn't also playing defensive tackle. And the head coach doesn't jump on the field every once and a while to run a play as a running back – *even if he used to be one*. Are you catching my drift?

Each position knows what they do, stays in their lane, sticks to what they are best at, and relies on the others on the team to do the same. So when you're building your championship Profit Team, consider developing and drafting a few key positions.

Depending on where you are in your build and what revenue benchmark you're currently in, the names or roles of these positions may change. Keep in mind that your current revenue benchmark will also determine your need to outsource each, or potentially bring each position in-house.

The structure of your profit players, and your overall business finance team, is crucial for driving business growth and essential for creating a scalable, sustainable, and sellable venture. There's no one-size-fits-all solution to creating the perfect structure, so you'll need to decide which approach works best for where you are, *and* where you want to go.

Factors like industry, company size, location, working models (centralized, decentralized, remote, or office-based), and outsourcing versus in-house all influence the structure you design. For instance, smaller businesses might only need a fractional CFO and some outsourced support staff like bookkeeping and accounting. Medium-sized businesses typically bring the outsourced roles in-house and start to develop a small finance department, handling accounting, account management, AP/AR, and other financial functions.

Larger companies, on the other hand, will of course require finance specialists for core functions. This can be anything from an experienced CFO or risk management specialist to accountants, controllers, treasury managers, and tax strategists, as well as those versed in mergers and acquisitions. They might even have teams aligned with specific business units to support key stakeholders and act as strategic partners.

In terms of process, smaller businesses often have a lean finance team of generalists, where each member handles multiple roles. Medium-sized companies tend to have a dedicated team of specialists in various finance processes, and larger corporations are structured with managers, department heads, and directors overseeing several functions.

So, when structuring your finance team and drafting the players you need, it's essential to have alignment with your business goals, revenue size, and operational needs.

The All-Star Players on Team Profit

Let's talk about a few positions, whether in-house, outsourced, or fractional players that almost every business needs.

First up, the **bookkeeper**. This is like the guy in the booth who reviews the plays when a referee throws a flag. The bookkeeper ensures all financial transactions are accurately recorded, keeping your financial playbook organized, up-to-date, detailed, current, and making sure that every penny is accounted for.

They make sure financials are accurate by recording transactions, keeping records organized, preparing reports when requested, and ensuring consistency through various reports. Bookkeepers operate with a historical component and are not the ones deciding on game-day strategies or calling routes. This is one of the first hires that should be made in any business. Every other position builds off of this one.

Next up is an all-star player, the **tax strategist**. They're like the quarterback, calling the shots when it comes to taxes, ensuring your business plays by the rules, and most importantly makes sure you're maximizing all of the deductions and credits available to you.

If you're aiming to grow your business and boost profitability, you can't send all of your cash to the IRS. Many entrepreneurs think that hiring or outsourcing to a traditional accountant to handle the taxes will be just fine, but I want to caution you it might not be the best approach.

Here's the thing: not all accountants or accounting firms are created equal. Some might just crunch the numbers without truly understanding your business and the host of specific deductions you might be able to take advantage of – you need someone who can do both.

I have seen many founders lose hundreds of thousands of dollars (and even millions of dollars) by missing this step and paying more in taxes than necessary. If you only meet with your accountant once, *after* your fiscal year has ended, you are operating in a reactive state and are not proactively planning your taxes.

A tax strategist is not a tax preparer. A tax strategist will go beyond basic accounting and perform an analysis on each aspect of your business with the goal to understand your business needs, advise on potential deductions, and ask questions to make sure you're not leaving anything on the table.

Because every business is different, there's no one-size-fits-all tax strategy. That's why having a financial professional who specializes in tax strategy on your Profit Team can be a game changer when it comes to maximizing profits.

Often, entrepreneurs think they can't afford this role, but truthfully you can't afford *not* to have one. When done correctly, it's a self-liquidating expense as a strategist maximizes deductions, reduces risk, and saves you endless time by keeping up with the 6,871 pages of the IRS code. Their expertise and approach to tax mitigation could make a *significant* difference in your bottom line.

Next on the line, you have the **CFO (chief financial officer)**. They're the mastermind behind your financial game plan, analyzing data, crafting strategies, and providing guidance to lead your team to victory. They are designing winning plays and adjusting tactics as the game progresses.

Whether they're a fractional CFO or full time, they're absolutely vital for any organization. As the head of finance and accounting, the CFO carries the weight of overseeing the financial operations of the organization and setting its strategic direction. They're the ones ultimately calling the shots on how the company's financial resources are managed.

The CFO is the head coach of team profit. They need to constantly monitor the organization's financial health and adjust course as needed to keep things sailing smoothly. Depending on the size and structure of your business, they may also be building and maintaining key relationships with banks, financial institutions, private investors, and venture capital – all of which come in handy when funding or capital is needed.

But here's the thing: even the most seasoned, experienced CFO can't navigate the field alone. They need top-notch finance and accounting players to provide them with timely, relevant information to make informed decisions and call the plays to keep the company going in the right direction. It's all about having that all-star team to back them up and ensure the organization stays on target.

Over on the 50-yard line of the field, you have the **business advisor**. This is an experienced mentor who acts as a general manager of team profit navigating the overall strategy of your business and can help you focus on successfully running your Profit Playbook.

They bring valuable insights, experience, and wisdom to the table, helping you navigate challenges and make smart strategic decisions. They're the seasoned business veteran who shares their expertise, advises on decisions, and guides you through tough or unavoidable critical challenges or situations.

A business advisor is someone who is versatile in business, has a depth of knowledge, and understands various aspects of a company. An advisor can integrate into, and offer support across, different functions, such as sales, HR, finance, and marketing.

By offering their expertise, they can fill in the gaps in a business, help increase speed of execution, and reduce expenses by providing strategic solutions.

Bringing in a business advisor can be a game changer for getting your business back on track, or helping you condense time and soar through growth benchmarks. Not only can they help address any critical issues in your business, but they can also offer a fresh perspective on new opportunities, revenue, or markets to grow your business.

It's crucial to find a head coach who isn't afraid to challenge you, even if there's pushback. A healthy relationship will involve open communication, where they provide candid opinions and recommendations.

Even if you don't always act on their suggestions, an advisor committed to your success will offer impartial, honest advice even if it challenges your beliefs or requires you to change. A successful relationship will require some humility, a willingness to learn, and sometimes even the decision to let go of past ideas, beliefs, or ego – all in an effort to grow, expand, and evolve.

All right, this next starting position isn't technically on the finance team, so let's call it special teams. Even though it's not a financial role, it's such a critical role that I see entrepreneurs miss that I have to at least touch on it. Most likely, unless you own a law firm, are in private equity, run a hedge fund, or are doing over $25 million in revenue, you probably don't need your own in-house counsel, but having a relationship with a **business attorney** is critical as you navigate through growth and scale.

It's worth repeating so I'll say it again: having a solid relationship with a business attorney is absolutely crucial. Often we think of them only being there to handle legal matters; but they can also help you avoid risk.

As time goes on, your business lawyer becomes an invaluable asset. As they get to know you, your business's needs, and the goals you have for its growth (or ultimate exit), they can provide recommendations to improve different areas of your business.

Love them or hate them – and most people fall into the latter category – contracts are the backbone of any business relationship, whether with customers, employees, vendors, independent contractors, or suppliers. Your lawyer can ensure these agreements provide the highest level of protection for you and your business. Whether it's including proper nondisclosure, noncompete, non-solicitation agreements, or non-disparagement clauses, there are endless options available for your protection, and your business attorney will determine which are best for you.

They can also review supplier contracts and licensing agreements, review or recommend proprietary assets and IP, as well as a host of other items to determine what's in your best interest. This is particularly crucial if you're entering into business in a partnership, or with family or a friend; having clear, written terms can prevent lawsuits and massive conflicts down the road.

Okay, so now that we have covered the starting positions and even special teams, how do all of these players run the plays? Well, your financial reports – rich with metrics and KPIs – make up the Profit Playbook guiding your overall winning strategy.

One thing I want to point out is that your **Profit Playbook** spends less time looking back on the past and more time looking ahead at what should happen *next*.

Let's take a look at how everything comes together from the start of this book to put together your own Profit Playbook.

Your Profit Playbook

In Part 1 of this book **More Revenue Now**, we laid the foundation for the importance of revenue generation and explored strategies for improving sales, diversifying income streams, and optimizing customer relationships. Let's take a moment to reflect on the foundation of revenue that you have built.

1 **Sales Revenue:** What are your current main sources of revenue, and how can you optimize, increase, or expand them based on the strategies outlined?

2 **Customer Acquisition:** Do you currently have a customer acquisition strategy, and how effectively are you using it to increase customers?

3 **Doing More with Less:** Can you increase AOV and/or BF to maximize sales revenue without acquiring new customers? Are there any lower performing products/services that can be eliminated?

4 **Making Price Irrelevant:** Evaluate your customer service process. Are there areas for improvement that could lead to increased sales volume, customer retention, or efficiency?

5 **Converting More Customers:** Are there Sniper Strategies you can leverage for greater exposure, market awareness, or increased conversions? How can this create greater viability and increase revenue?

6 List your top three **KPIs** related to **REVENUE:**

Your Profit Playbook

In Part 2 of this book, **More Profit Now** we shift from revenue generation to profit maximization with strategies for cost control, optimizing operations, and making strategic decisions that create a more efficient, profitable business by focusing on your metrics that matter most to success.

1 **Expense Allocations:** What are the top three areas where you could reduce costs without sacrificing quality or customer satisfaction?

2 **Profit Optimization:** Which of your products, services, or customers have the highest profit margins, and how can you focus more resources on these areas?

3 **Strategic Decision-Making:** Reflect on a recent business decision that had a significant impact on your profit. What did you learn from this experience, and how will it influence your future decisions?

4 **Process Efficiency:** Are there any processes or systems that need to be implemented that can make your profit become more sustainable and predictable?

5 **Team Profit Players:** How are the players on your profit team? Are there any positions you need to hire or outsource in order to consistently focus on scaling your profit?

6 List your top three **KPIs** related to **PROFIT:**

Accounting for Profit

Now, why am I including accounting methods in this book? Because I know you want to build a scalable, sustainable, and sellable business, so there are some basic accounting nuances to understand in order to determine what approach is best for your business. Entrepreneurs often start out using the cash accounting method, and then don't know if, or when, it may be better to switch to accrual accounting. And frankly, how would you? We don't know what we don't know. I didn't know either, until I knew. Funny how that works.

There are two main processes for accounting: **cash accounting** or **accrual accounting**. You'll use one or the other:

- Cash accounting: Income isn't added until you've actually received the payment, and expenses aren't deducted until they're paid.
- Accrual accounting: This type counts income and expenses when they occur, not when they're paid.

Cash accounting, in short, is keeping track of your finances based on when money actually comes in or goes out. So if you receive payment from a customer or pay a bill, you record that transaction at that exact moment. This is where most small businesses start because it's pretty straightforward; it reflects the cash flow of your business.

Accrual accounting, on the other hand, is more about matching revenues and expenses with the time they're earned or incurred, regardless of when cash changes hands. This means you record transactions when goods are delivered or services are performed, not just when the money moves in or out of your account.

I remember wondering why I didn't know about this sooner. And why is accrual accounting considered better for understanding the overall health of a business?

Here's what I learned then, and now know to be true. Accrual accounting gives you a more accurate picture of your financial situation because it reflects all the economic activities of your business, not just the ones tied to cash. It helps you see the full scope of your revenues and expenses, even if cash hasn't been exchanged yet. This gives you a real-time view of your sales and helps you track your performance accurately.

If you have expenses like rent or utilities that you pay in advance, accrual accounting ensures you record those expenses when they're incurred, not just when the bill comes due. This helps you manage your cash flow more effectively and plan for future expenses.

Overall it provides a more comprehensive and more accurate view of your business's financial health and gives you a full picture of your finances, rather than just focusing on the cash flow aspect. That's why many businesses, especially larger ones, prefer to use accrual accounting to make informed decisions and plan for the future.

There are approximately 34 million small businesses in the United States, and about 64% of them try to do their own bookkeeping. That number is extremely high, especially when you factor in that 68% of small business owners surveyed feel they aren't knowledgeable when it comes to business finance or accounting.

Having an experienced bookkeeper, either in-house or outsourced, will not only help keep your finances organized and your reports in order, but it pays for itself. Delegating this time-consuming task to a pro frees up your time so you can spend it proactively growing your business.

Small businesses are defined by the IRS as businesses that generate $26 million or less in annual revenue. Most small businesses can generally choose whether they want to use cash accounting or the accrual method. However, large businesses and corporations over that amount can be required to use the accrual method.

Now, why does this matter?

Although cash accounting might seem simpler, accrual accounting offers a more accurate snapshot of a company's financial standing, providing real-time insights into your company's finances. For that reason, most businesses can benefit from it to manage cash flow, anticipate financial obligations, and make more informed decisions about future investments or projects, giving you a clearer understanding of your financial situation and helping you plan for the road ahead.

Running your business with this accounting method over cash accounting can be easier, and better, overall. It will take some time to transition over to it; however, lean on the players on your Profit Team to identify whether this is a good strategy for you and your growth as you continue to build sustainable cash flow and create a scalable business.

Remember, each player on your financial team plays a specific role in executing that playbook effectively. The tax strategist ensures compliance and maximizes savings, the CFO develops and executes strategic initiatives, the bookkeeper maintains accurate records, the advisor provides invaluable advice and support, and the attorney ensures protection and mitigates risk.

Together, they form a cohesive unit, working in sync to drive your business toward success. Just as a championship sports team relies on teamwork, strategy, and execution to win, the players on your Profit Team use their expertise to make informed decisions, manage resources efficiently, and position you and your business for long-term success.

If you have any questions about building the right Profit Team or would like to be connected with professionals who are experienced, trained, and certified to help you and your business grow, go to **www .candyvalentino.com**. You can find lists of professionals who can help you increase your profitability and more efficiently move toward creating a sustainable and successful business.

Here's the magic to all of this. Your finances aren't just numbers and ratios. They hold the key to your freedom. By measuring what matters, consistently holding your State of the Union meetings, taking time to uncover the profit hiding in your business, and being intentional about recruiting the right players on your Profit Team – you will create more profit now. You'll also be setting yourself up not only to potentially exit your business, but you'll end up creating more freedom for yourself.

I don't know any entrepreneur who doesn't want some more of that, so let's jump into the final part of this book and look at how you can create More Freedom Now.

PART III

More Freedom NOW

CHAPTER 10

Four Exits Every Founder Needs to Make

How would you make business decisions now if you knew you were going to exit later?

"**M**y husband wants to retire, but I don't know if I can," she said to me over Zoom with concern in her voice. While that might be an exciting proposition to some, it can invoke fear in entrepreneurs.

If I were new to understanding this paradox that entrepreneurs struggle with, or didn't completely identify with what she was saying, I would have asked for more context. But this challenge is common for entrepreneurs, especially successful ones.

Erin built her firm from the ground up, turning it into a multi-million-dollar company with 50-plus employees and clients in every state. She has such depth, strength, and brilliance, and is completely down-to-earth and unaware of how she embodies each. She operates with so much ease and grace, it was almost as if she thought what she accomplished to this point was as common and unassuming as running daily errands.

The interesting thing about success is that it can bring an overwhelming sense of responsibility. Erin found herself buried in the day-to-day operations of the business, constantly juggling tasks, putting out fires, and wearing multiple hats to keep things running smoothly.

After years of pouring her heart and soul into building this company, she approached a certain point in her life where she and her husband began to entertain the idea of retirement. She knew that if she wanted her company to continue thriving – *and* if she wanted to enjoy some freedom in even a semi-retired state – she needed to make a change.

That's when we began our work together. Some of the strategies I took her through are those that I have discussed in this book. We looked at scaling her profit, optimizing her operations, developing better processes, and started to work through the critical exits every founder needs to make in order to have more freedom.

It may feel like we're getting ahead of ourselves – trying to plan your exit before achieving more revenue growth – but think of it this way. If you set off without a plan, it's like getting in the car without having a destination. Unless you're just in it for the scenic drive, you've got to know where you're heading.

It becomes *critically* important once you learn that **82% of businesses live and die with their owners**.[1] That means that if you want to make it into the 18% who manage to make the final exit, you've got to lead your business with intention.

It goes back to the very first words of this chapter. How would you make business decisions *now* knowing you wanted to exit *later*?

Entrepreneurs often focus on the final exit – selling their business for a profit – as the ultimate goal. However, there are a few exits you will likely need to make before reaching that point.

Transitioning from working *in* the front lines of the business to working *on* the systems and processes of the business – from delegating responsibilities to empowering others to lead, even to relinquishing control – exiting these four roles in your business enables you to pave the way for a successful final exit when the time is right.

THE FOUR EXITS EVERY FOUNDER NEEDS TO MAKE

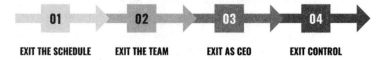

01	02	03	04
EXIT THE SCHEDULE	EXIT THE TEAM	EXIT AS CEO	EXIT CONTROL

Step 1: Exit the Schedule

Exiting the schedule will allow you to work on building the team who builds the product, instead of building the product.

For Erin, exiting her schedule was a daunting thought. She had become so accustomed to being hands-on in every aspect of her business that the idea of stepping back was both terrifying and exhilarating. But she also understood that to truly move forward and grow further, she needed to let go of the day-to-day minutiae and develop her team to take the reins.

Together, we developed a plan to streamline operations and identify key roles to hire and responsibilities that could be delegated. We identified which employees could take further ownership of their roles and those who weren't going to grow with her in this next phase. It wasn't easy. Erin struggled with feelings of guilt and apprehension as she truly cared about her business and her people. But with each passing day, she grew more confident in her decision and rested in the knowledge that this was the best path for her to take.

Embracing effective delegation isn't just about freeing up your time, though that is certainly a significant factor. It's also about fostering a culture of trust and empowerment within your organization so that you can build better operational efficiency and have less owner dependency.

By trusting your team with greater responsibilities, you show that you believe in their abilities and value their contributions. And in return, most employees will rise to the occasion. You'd be surprised how many times I've seen underperforming employees become an overperforming team when the owner stepped out of the way and allowed them to demonstrate their commitment and dedication to the business.

As Erin gradually stepped out of the day-to-day grind, she was no longer stuck in endless to-do lists and constant firefighting. She was able to focus her energy on the bigger picture and create greater opportunities for the business. By giving herself space and bandwidth, she was able to grow top-line revenue and increase profitability within one quarter of making this change, giving her renewed optimism and greater confidence.

If you find yourself entrenched in the day-to-day operations of your business, you are not alone. This commonly happens to great founders who are high-performing, deeply competent, and so dang good at what they do that they forget to stop and duplicate themselves so they can delegate their role to others.

Embracing **effective delegation is the first key to stepping into a sustainable business, and stepping out of your time-consuming job**. The *Harvard Business Review* stated that one of the most difficult transitions for leaders to make is the shift from *doing* to *leading*.[2]

While it may seem difficult, increasing your impact in your business will cause you to face an unavoidable paradox. In order to get to the next level in your build, the rule to remember is this: the *who* cannot be *you*.

Hopeful and early-stage entrepreneurs typically start with the spirit of "I can do it!" But the traits you needed to start the business are not the same as the ones you'll need to sustain the business.

If you want to become part of the 9% who creates sustainable success in business, instead of asking, "How can I do this?" you must ask, "Who can I get to do this?"

This leadership paradox of being more essential and less involved is required for your continued growth. Staying involved and being essential is not the same any more than being busy and being productive are equal. This concept will require a shift in mindset from being hands-on in every aspect of the work, to strategically empowering others to take on responsibilities and make decisions.

On the surface, this may sound like common sense, but common sense isn't always common practice. Often we will intellectually understand a concept, but that doesn't mean we apply it.

To complete the first exit, mastering effective delegation is vital. Just know that it's commonly one of the hardest skills for great entrepreneurs to master.

The fastest way for an entrepreneur to become their own glass ceiling is to refuse to learn how to properly delegate.

Delegation is not a sign of weakness; instead, it's a sign of a strong leader.

Here are five tips to effective delegation and how to use this with your team:

Tip 1: Define the Desired Outcome

Simply telling someone they are doing a project or task for you isn't delegation. Handing off work to your team should always come with proper context and clarity as well as why this is important or how it ties to the business's, the team's, or the department's goal. "You've got to have real clarity of the objective," says Harvard Business School professor Kevin Sharer.[3]

Before anyone starts working on a project, they should know what they need to complete and by when, including the metrics you'll use to measure the success of their work.

Personally, I think one of the easiest and simplest ways to do this is with a SMART goal framework.

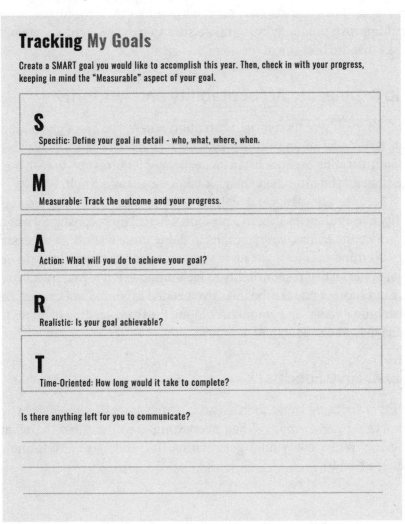

Tracking My Goals

Create a SMART goal you would like to accomplish this year. Then, check in with your progress, keeping in mind the "Measurable" aspect of your goal.

S
Specific: Define your goal in detail - who, what, where, when.

M
Measurable: Track the outcome and your progress.

A
Action: What will you do to achieve your goal?

R
Realistic: Is your goal achievable?

T
Time-Oriented: How long would it take to complete?

Is there anything left for you to communicate?

Tip 2: Choose the Right Team Members

To effectively delegate as a leader, it's crucial to match the right task with the right team member. Match tasks with team members based on their strengths, weaknesses, and preferences.

For instance, if a task requires collaboration, don't delegate it to someone who prefers working alone. After identifying tasks for delegation, consider discussing them with your team. Allow team members to choose tasks they're most interested in.

This approach not only helps in task allocation but also encourages greater engagement, because they'll feel more empowered and committed to contribute to tasks they specifically find meaningful. In addition, it can increase trust and commitment with your employees and improve productivity, so make sure to pair the right people with tasks that are best suited for them.

Tip 3: Delegate Accountability and Authority

I'm sure you've experienced a situation where you were given a task but didn't feel in control to make decisions on your own. It's more than frustrating because it can create delays, requires you to seek more assistance, and ultimately the task takes longer as a result.

Leaders who struggle to delegate not only tasks but also responsibility may find themselves in a position where they're constantly having to answer questions, which results in doing more work than necessary.

It's important to create an environment where the person you delegated the task or responsibility to feels empowered to make decisions, ask questions, and take the initiative needed to get the work done. This fosters ownership and autonomy among the team, leading to increased efficiency and productivity.

Tip 4: Give Feedback

Is there anything worse than a leader who blames the employee when something goes wrong? When everything goes right, it's the team's success. When everything goes wrong, it's your fault. Welcome to being a leader!

Don't make the mistake of this "hit and run" leadership tactic known as delegate and blame. Effective delegation requires you to check the work you delegated, confirm what's right or correct, and provide any feedback on what needs changed or improved when handling the task going forward.

Remember, "check in," don't "check out."

Tip 5: Recognize the Effort

Reward and recognize the behaviors you want to continue. When the person you delegated a task or project to accomplishes the work, show sincere appreciation and always make sure to recognize the specific things they did well.

So often, people go through their lives feeling that their efforts, their value, or their talents are invisible. When you take the simple yet important step of taking note of the things someone on your team did right, you're helping them become more successful. Sometimes the smallest things can create significant results – not just in your team, their performance, and effectiveness, but it can also create an impact on the person that extends far beyond the workplace.

Now that you've mastered effective delegation and successfully exited the schedule, it's time to exit the team. For Erin, she had been a hands-on manager for so long, now it was time for her to transform into a true CEO.

Step 2: Exit the Team

Exiting from the team and stepping into a true CEO role will allow you to work on building the company, instead of building the team.

A lot of founders think they're a CEO. It might even say it in their bio, but they're actually overqualified managers or operators still working in the business. Managers are key roles that are needed for most businesses to function well, and you may very well have been serving in that role out of desperation or need. However, building a scalable, sustainable company will require you to duplicate yourself and eventually exit the team.

However, like I shared in Chapter 1, the intention behind every business is different. You might *not* want to exit the team, and that's okay. For some entrepreneurs, going to work every day in the business that you've built could be the reason why you started on this journey to begin with. So why would you ever want to change that? Well, you don't have to.

Remember, technically nothing is required. There are many reasons why you may want to stay right where you are. Maybe you enjoy what you do, maybe it works for you and your family, or maybe it serves a different need and you don't have any desire to sell your business – meaning one day you will either close your doors or have an asset sale.

But maybe you want to architect a scalable, sustainable, sellable business and have the intention to exit one day. Maybe you want all of your hard work to create a payoff at the end and you dream of sitting at the table signing papers, having your very own capital exit. If that's your goal but you don't know your options or how to get there, I'm here for that, too, so let's continue.

The role of a great manager is critically important. The business world has been so enamored with the focus of leadership, it's almost as if management became a word to detest. No one wants to be known as a manager these days; instead they want to be called a leader. But the words are not the same, nor are their functions.

It's risky to separate management from leadership. When there is leadership without effective management, momentum becomes stalled and stagnant. On the other hand, management without effective leadership can become uninspired and lack collaboration.

If you're naturally an exceptional manager, you'll need to shift your focus to evolve into the role of an exceptional leader. But I would assume you already possess some innate leadership abilities, or you wouldn't have come this far in your business.

Great Leaders Take Risks; Great Managers Control Risk

Great leaders are intentional about seeing the long-term visions, the big picture, and stay relentless in achieving it; great managers work on the short-term goals to achieve that long-term vision. Leaders can work without recognition; managers need to be refocused, rewarded, and recognized along the way. Leaders often have a desire to always be learning new skills and increasing their knowledge; managers are more inclined to refine their skills and deepen their knowledge.

An article published by Texas A&M University stated, "While leadership and management sometimes overlap, it is not always guaranteed."[4] Many managers will do what they need to do to complete their tasks and fulfill their responsibilities. They don't commonly push themselves or their teams to go above and beyond. Leaders, on the other hand, view every opportunity as a chance to grow, learn, and excel. They motivate others around them, and inspire their team to strive and grow.

Can a manager be a great leader? Yes, they can, but most aren't. Can a leader be a great manager? Yes, but typically they aren't, either. They are more than just two different roles; they are really two different people in the way they think, act, and view success. Successful leaders are more vision-oriented, while successful managers are more detail-oriented.

It's important to look at the differences between a great manager and a great leader for three reasons:

1. To give yourself permission to leave behind the role you were once good at.
2. To know what qualities to look for in the hire you make to replace yourself.
3. To determine what qualities you want to enhance or adopt in order to transition into the next-level leader you're becoming.

Henri Fayol was a French mining engineer, mining executive, and author in the late 1800s. He is also known as the father of Modern Management Theory. All of the concepts and strategies we have today seem to go back to his work over 100 years ago. He gave a new perception on the concept of management that can be applied to all levels of management and every department.

Fayol created the Five Functions of Management to help clarify and define the role a manager plays in business. Those five functions are:

- Planning and the ability to create things like a budget
- Organizing a workable company structure that includes chain of command and role definition

- Commanding and getting the most from people
- Coordinating departments so they know the responsibilities of their team
- Controlling and measuring how a team is doing against a budget or performance goals

Henri Fayol also created the 14 principles of management that identified the skills he determined were needed for someone to become an exceptional manager and do it well. His principles still inspire a lot of the management theory we implement today.[5]

When we look at the differences of the core principles of management and compare them to the role of leadership, there are some stark differences.

A good leader has vision, integrity, and empathy. They delegate, connect, and communicate to understand. They naturally motivate and are influential to others.

A great leader has fortitude, resolve, and relentless persistence. They have the ability to remain calm, stay engaged, and in the face of adversity, still inspire others around them. They embrace challenges, take responsibility in crisis, and look at problems head on.

In business, there will be a time where a good leader will be given an opportunity to become a great one.

A *good* leader is often created through training or experience. Good leadership can be taught, observed, or learned. But a *great* leader? Great leaders are developed by facing adversity and taking on challenges. A good leader, when faced with the right obstacles, has the opportunity to be a great leader, because great leaders aren't created from education. They are risen from circumstance.

If you've been a great *manager* in your business, stepping out of that role and becoming a great *leader* will require you to make new decisions, ones that create new behaviors, that create new habits, that create new results. Stepping into the role of CEO can be difficult and lonely. The stakes are high, the demand is great, so your vision and purpose have to be greater.

This was such a challenging transition for me. Starting out in business with seven employees on day one of opening, I was immediately a manager. Talk about being thrown into the middle of the ocean to learn how to swim. Although I had the title of president, I was also so young that the United States had only just allowed me to vote for the president of the country. Could I manage people? Yes, I had been doing that since I was a little kid at my dad's garage. But lead people? Definitely not. I couldn't even order a glass of wine at the bar; how could I lead anyone? Be a CEO? I mean aren't all leaders and CEOs outgoing, extroverted, and super-confident? Not to mention all men with trust funds and Ivy League educations?

I certainly don't fit into that category. And quite honestly, I have no idea how I kept employees in the beginning of building my first business. No one is born ready. And there is no trust fund or expensive education that can guarantee you'll ever be a great leader.

Nevertheless, to get where I wanted to go, I knew it needed to happen. So I read books on leadership, went to leadership events, and attended seminars on how to be a good leader because I knew taking on the role of CEO was going to require it.

Great leaders aren't created from education. They are risen from circumstance.

Do you have what it takes to be the CEO of your company? That might sound like a crazy question to ask, but some of the most successful founders I know, when asked that question, have surprisingly but honestly answered "no."

But how do you know? Maybe like me you have a picture in your mind of what a CEO is supposed to look like and a list of characteristics and personality traits they possess. So I think the better question to ask is, "What makes a great CEO?"

Let's take a look at a research project that spanned 10 years to find out. Four researchers – Elena Lytkina Botelho, Kim Rosen Powell, Stephen Kincaid, and Dina Wang – conducted a detailed analysis of 17,000 executives for what they called the CEO Genome Project.[6] After reviewing the in-depth assessments of each executive, including each leader's career history, business results, and behavioral patterns, they uncovered something surprising.

There is a large disconnect between what we *think* makes for an ideal CEO versus what *actually* leads to being successful in the role.

CEOs need to exude charisma, project confidence, and have an education pedigree to be successful, right? The 10-year study proved these widely held assumptions wrong.

You'd think extroverts made the list of the most successful chief executive officers. Nope. Introverts are more likely to surpass expectations of their boards and investors. It was very interesting to learn that educational pedigree (or lack thereof) was in no way correlated to performance. They found that 93% of the high-performing CEOs in the study didn't have an Ivy League education, and 8% of them didn't graduate from college at all.

The most important part of their research was the discovery that successful chief executives tend to demonstrate four specific behaviors that prove to be critical to performance. These behaviors are going to sound deceptively simple, but success is found when they are implemented consistently, which is a challenge for many leaders.

The four specific behaviors that the most successful CEOs of the 17,000 studied exhibited were:

1. **Speed of execution:** They're decisive and execute on decision-making. They realize they can't wait for all of the perfect information or the perfect timing and know that a wrong decision is often better than no decision at all. When faced with a decision, they make it faster, earlier, and with greater confidence. They do this consistently, even when faced with uncertainty, incomplete information, or unfamiliar situations. This behavior makes an average CEO 12 times more likely to be a great CEO.

2. **Engage to impact:** The key is that once a clear course is set, they actively involve employees (and other stakeholders) for their buy-in. They have a keen insight into priorities and balance, bringing everyone together with unrelenting focus on delivering business results. They actively involve themselves to make a difference and actively make an effort to understand what's important to everyone involved, bringing together and aligning others toward creating something valuable and beneficial. They are good at engagement, giving everyone at the table a voice, but not a vote. They listen and solicit views, but do not default to making decisions by consensus. The top-performing CEOs are also composed and calm under pressure.

3. **Adapt to challenges:** They are proactive in adjusting and changing as needed but keep their eye on the long-term vision of the organization. They are mindful of future goals and stay focused on the desired outcomes, not the short-term challenges that present themselves. They view mistakes as opportunities to learn and improve and continue to forge ahead during adversity. They regularly look at broad information and scan diverse sources of data to find relevance in information that may at first seem unrelated. As a result, they are almost intuitive in their function and can sense a change earlier than most. This enables them to make strategic moves to take advantage of the situation. CEOs who excel at adapting are 6.7 times more likely to be high-performing in their role.

4. **Ability to deliver:** As boring as it may sound, the ability to produce results was possibly the most powerful of the four essential CEO behaviors. They deliver results in a reliable fashion, steadily following through on commitments. They reliably fulfill their promises and obligations time after time and consistently produce outcomes that can be trusted. Reliability is paramount in being successful, and with this single behavior alone, you're 15 times more likely to be a high-performing CEO.

The key to consistently delivering results depends on setting realistic expectations, having proper organization and planning skills, as well as establishing business management systems. The most successful CEOs the team researched all created a cadence of meetings, dashboards of metrics, clear accountability, and multiple channels for monitoring performance and making rapid course corrections.

Most importantly, they surrounded themselves with strong teams, moving decisively and upgrading talent when needed. They set the bar really high and focused on performance.

When you exit the team, you're truly stepping out of the managerial functions of the business and you're overseeing direction, vision, and growth as CEO.

Erin had everything it took to be a successful leader and CEO. We worked on creating processes and systems so that she could truly step into her role, as well as hire any additional C-suite players she needed (COO, CFO) so she could rely on her team to handle tasks efficiently and effectively without needing her constant oversight.

Through it all, Erin navigated these first two exits with grace and determination. Each step brought her closer to her ultimate goal of retirement while ensuring the continued success of her business. And as she embarked on this new chapter of her life, she did so with the knowledge that she had built something truly remarkable – and that the best was yet to come.

Step 3: Exit as CEO

Exiting from the role of CEO and stepping into the role of board chair (or a similar role) will allow you to provide strategic guidance, instead of managing daily operations.

You're now at a point where you've got an incredible, flourishing team on the frontlines. You hired effective managers, developed leaders, and ensured that operational systems, policies, and procedures are being implemented while others are handling the day-to-day.

You're now the CEO, captain of your ship, envisioning what's next for the business, looking into opportunities for growth and exploring potential directions for you and your business to go.

Where could you possibly go from here? For you, maybe this is where you wanted to be. Maybe you're going to ride this wave until you can't anymore. Maybe you're waiting until one of your children shows interest. There's nothing wrong with either. It's about knowing what you want, and realizing it's okay to have it.

But if you want to relinquish this role at some point, want to create passive income, or to successfully have a capital exit, you may have two more steps to go.

Sometimes founders will replace themselves as CEO to take a board seat as chair. This involves replacing yourself for the last and final position inside the business while you still maintain power and possibly full control of the company. While it's true that exiting the role of CEO to take a board seat isn't a common step for most entrepreneurs, there may be some alternative options to consider.

If your business industry or model isn't structured in a way that having a board would make sense, perhaps you consider stepping into an advisory/consulting or emerita role. As an advisor or a consultant, you could offer strategic guidance and mentorship to the leadership team, leveraging your experience and knowledge of the company to support its growth and success. An emerita role may allow you to retain an honorary title and stay connected to the company's legacy, serving as a respected ambassador for the brand.

While these roles may not be as commonly pursued as taking a board seat, they offer opportunities to stay engaged and contribute to the businesses in a meaningful way even after stepping down as CEO.

In 2021, I had the pleasure of interviewing Rick Steele at one of my Founders Business Boardroom events. Rick is founder of the billion-dollar industry disrupter Select Blinds. He said that regardless of the company he builds, it is always his number-one goal to fire himself as CEO.

Seasoned, successful entrepreneurs like Rick know that you can easily become the bottleneck in your growth and scale. And if you're willing to lose the entrepreneurial ego, hiring a CEO to run your company may be the exact next step you need to take in order for the business to reach its greatest potential.

A more famous example of this is Jeff Bezos. In 2021, Bezos made the move from CEO to executive chair in order to spend more time on his various ventures and philanthropic endeavors.[7] Despite taking on a different role within the company, Bezos's impact at Amazon remains substantial with his leadership role in heading the board. As its largest individual shareholder and mentor to the new CEO, Bezos is poised to have significant influence over the company for years to come.

Step 4: Exit Control

Exiting control, or your role on the board, while still maintaining ownership of the company will allow you to work on new ventures while still having equity and income.

The fourth and final exit step is when you exit control. This exit is a great option for entrepreneurs who have built a successful business and are ready to enjoy the fruits of their labor. Having equity in the company, but not responsibility, can have its benefits.

Many founders may find it challenging to relinquish control of their company, but doing so can open doors to new opportunities and ventures. By maintaining even partial ownership of the company while transitioning out of day-to-day operations and governance, you can pursue new ventures or interests without being tied down by the demands of running a business. This can result in passive income and the ability to explore fresh ideas, or simply enjoy more freedom, all while benefiting from the income generated by your original company, which ultimately leads to greater fulfillment and financial freedom.

Steve Jobs was famously fired from Apple in 1985, even though he owned 8–10% of the stock at that time. He later had his own remarkable comeback story, but this shows how you can have an equity interest in a company without being involved. Although Jobs was removed from his position, much like Jack Dorsey, founder of Twitter (now X), and Travis Kalanick, founder of Uber, there are other stories where founders *chose* to leave while retaining an equity position.

The best example of this is Bill Gates. He relinquished his position as CEO of Microsoft in 2000, yet continued to hold a leadership position at Microsoft for two decades until 2020, when he eventually stepped down from the board. He still owns 1.3% of the company,[8] resulting in billions of dollars of income.

If you have a smaller business and don't have a board to formally exit from, there are still several ways you can relinquish control while retaining equity positions. You can identify potential successors within the organization and gradually hand over control while retaining ownership. Alternatively, you could establish a trust or holding company to manage the business, appointing trustees or managers to oversee operations while retaining ownership rights. Another option is to reduce your position and sell a minority stake in the company.

Just as there are endless ways to build a business, there are endless ways to structure your exit. It's all about finding what works best for you and your long-term vision.

Exiting control doesn't have to mean you are stepping away from the company; you're just stepping away from the responsibilities. The income from your shares or ownership in the company can become purely passive, allowing you to pursue any passion or project you want.

These four exits can pave the path for you to create a roadmap for more freedom now and even give yourself permission to reclaim autonomy in your life. In the last chapter, "The Final Exit," I cover this pivotal and monumental transition to the ultimate exit. I break down what complexities to look for, what possibilities lie ahead, and how to leverage the exit principles to stack the odds in your favor to become part of the 9%. Let's continue walking this journey together.

CHAPTER 11

The Final Exit

Your exit will likely end up different than you expect, but it may end up being exactly what you need.

"Great, I look forward to seeing you on Thursday, Scott."

She hung up the receiver on her office phone and took a deep breath, the deepest one she had taken in over a year. She leaned back in her chair and without meaning to, she paused. A smile began to form on both sides of her mouth. "I can't believe I did it," she thought to herself, but quickly realized she whispered it aloud.

She had worked so incredibly hard at growing her business. She stayed focused and worked through the exact steps of building a scalable business. She read the books, worked with mentors, attended the seminars, and operated with intention from the beginning so that she could build to exit. She made smart decisions, and stayed diligent and resilient. She said no to so many things so that she could say yes to this one thing, and to a life beyond her wildest imagination.

She displayed unwavering discipline and commitment throughout the last two decades and although she wanted to quit so many times along the way, she didn't.

Through that perseverance, she finally attracted a buyer. She made it through the egregious due diligence period, and successfully navigated months of meetings without the team or thousands of clients finding out.

The final documents were being prepared, and all the lawyers were set. Now she had reached the 11th hour.

The moment finally arrived to initiate this pivotal move, only to find that unexpected challenges arose with financing. What seemed like a small change to the closing date ended up disrupting the entire deal. Those few days turned into a few weeks, which turned into a couple of months, and the buyer finally secured new financing.

A new closing date was scheduled. *Whew.* Although those 10 weeks felt like it took 10 years, it seemed to be the end of this rollercoaster ride. She found herself in the 11th hour again when she received that phone call.

She was mentally ready for this, excited even. And then just as she was about to approach the signing table, tragedy struck yet again. It was déjà vu. Only this time it wasn't the buyer's financing falling through; it was a spontaneous combustion in one of the buildings. A spark created an electrical fire and destroyed an entire building, as well as everything inside it, and caused the entire deal to burn to the ground with it.

She was me. Just like that, my second exit went up in smoke. *Literally.*

The reality is this: even when you do your best to do everything right, the final exit can be a challenging, emotional, and volatile process. The photo you capture inside the conference room shaking hands and smiling after the documents are signed doesn't tell the story of what it takes to get there.

Of course, a few acquisition stories feature sunshine and rainbows, a few successful mergers that happen with ease, but most are filled with a lot of hard work, dedication, and commitment to seeing it through to the end.

Regardless of where you are in your business right now – whether you're just starting out, growing your revenue, focusing on sustainability and profitability, or in the midst of scaling an enterprise that you dream will be acquired one day – there are five fundamental exit principles. These principles will give you the edge to make it to that signing table.

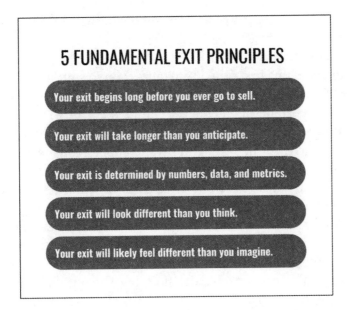

Exit Principle #1: Your Exit Begins Long Before You Ever Go to Sell

At its core, this first principle emphasizes the importance of strategic planning and foresight. It highlights the role of preparation in a successful business exit. The groundwork for a lucrative exit needs to be laid well in advance of the actual sale process. Rather than viewing the sale as a singular event, I encourage you to see it differently.

For the parents out there, imagine for a moment if you didn't raise your children for the first 18 years of their lives. You didn't send them to school or teach them the fundamentals of education. You didn't build a strong bond of nurturing or caring about them. Instead, your strategy was to hope that when they graduated and turned 18, they would have everything they needed to be successful, fully functioning adults without you having to do anything to help them become that way.

Leaving it all to chance wouldn't work too well. Nor would building a business with the hope of it becoming part of the 9% and having a scalable, sustainable, or sellable venture without having a clear plan in place.

The decisions you make now, and throughout the build of your business, will significantly impact its attractiveness to potential buyers when the time comes to exit.

Embracing this first principle requires you to shift from operating in a reactive state to being more proactive within the build. Even if the thought of an exit never entered your mind, there are a few things you can do now to give yourself the opportunity later.

It's not easy, but it is straightforward: adopt a long-term perspective and envision the desired outcome for your business exit from the outset. This involves setting clear goals, whether it's maximizing financial returns, ensuring a smooth transition, or preserving the company's legacy. Because building a business with the *intention* to sell changes everything. It forces a relentless focus on value creation from the beginning.

Imagine if every strategic decision, investment, and operational improvement you made were evaluated based on its potential impact on the company's value, but not now – later, and from the eyes of prospective *buyers*.

Planning for an exit is a long-term strategy that's best started well before you have any intention of doing so. It involves meticulous planning aimed at enhancing the business's bottom line, through diversifying revenue streams, solidifying customer relationships, fortifying intellectual property assets, and optimizing operational efficiency.

Financial discipline (which we will cover in depth later in this chapter) is also crucial in laying the foundation for a successful exit. Entrepreneurs must maintain clean financial records, maximize profitability, and demonstrate stable, sustainable growth to instill confidence in potential buyers and command the premium valuation you and your business deserves.

Imagine if you started building a talented management team a little earlier than you felt necessary. How could the decision to invest in talent development, succession planning, and leadership training strengthen your business now, and increase its value later?

Regularly assessing the business's exit readiness long before you "need" to will allow you to identify the business's strengths, weaknesses, and areas for improvement. And by conducting an annual comprehensive evaluation of key value drivers, risks, and potential impediments, your business will be prepared for a seamless transition when the time comes to sell.

"Your exit begins long before you ever go to sell" serves as a guiding principle for entrepreneurs embarking on the journey of building and eventually exiting a business. By internalizing this principle and incorporating it into your daily business practice, you can lay the groundwork for a successful exit that maximizes value. Through proactive planning, you'll be able to better navigate the complexities of business ownership with clarity and purpose, ultimately positioning yourself for a bigger and more rewarding exit.

Exit Principle #2: Your Exit Will Take Longer Than You Anticipate

"I can't wait to be sipping margs in Cabo next month." Entrepreneurs often think this way before they go through their first exit. If only it were that easy (sigh).

As much as I'd love to tell you that's the case, the reality of selling your business is far from a quick getaway. It's a prolonged journey, one that may extend for 12 or 24 months, or possibly even 36 depending on your size, industry, and structure of the deal.

Along the way, potential buyers may drop out, and the due diligence process can be more than a headache; it can actually be quite painful. And because I always shoot it straight, you even might think you're getting to the signing table only to find yourself going through the entire process multiple times before finally sealing the deal. So it's crucial to abandon any illusions of a 90-day sprint.

Just look at the transaction I shared with you in the beginning of this chapter. It took one year to get to the signing table with the first buyer, only for it to blow up. After that deal dissolved, it took almost another full year with the second buyer.

Selling your business is a marathon – it can be tough, draining, hard to finish, but the feeling you have when you cross the checkered flag at the 26.2-mile mark can also be exhalating and beyond worth it. And just like training for a marathon, the exit process can take a toll on your mental well-being. Preparation is key; the more groundwork you lay before entering the market, the smoother the ride will be when the going gets tough.

It's essential to seek professional advice from legal, financial, and tax experts to ensure a successful and legally compliant transaction.

The EXITS framework breaks down the complex process into a more digestible action plan.

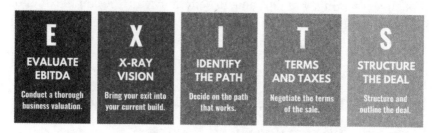

E	X	I	T	S
EVALUATE EBITDA	**X-RAY VISION**	**IDENTIFY THE PATH**	**TERMS AND TAXES**	**STRUCTURE THE DEAL**
Conduct a thorough business valuation.	Bring your exit into your current build.	Decide on the path that works.	Negotiate the terms of the sale.	Structure and outline the deal.

But before you work through the EXITS framework, there's some pre-work to do to set yourself up for the process.

Pre-exit Ramp: Prepare

Organize your financial records, ensure legal compliance, tighten up processes and systems, and tidy up any loose ends in your business.

With this prep work is in mind, it's time to dive into the EXITS framework.

E: EBITDA (Valuation of Business)

Understanding how EBITDA (Earnings Before Interest, Taxes, Depreciation, and Amortization) will, in most cases, have a significance impact on your overall valuation, is key. By having a thorough business valuation conducted – which may involve assessing your business's assets, cash flow, profitability, solvency, efficiency, market conditions, and comparable sales – you can gain knowledge on how valuable your business may be to a potential buyer. We'll get into key factors that can pay multiples on EBITDA later in the chapter.

X: X-Ray Vision

Having "X-ray vision" is seeing through surface-level decisions to understand how they can impact your future exit. It's about having foresight and planning ahead to ensure that the steps you take now align with your long-term business goals. How you make strategic decisions today will not only contribute to the present success and growth of your business, but can also set the stage for future sustainable success and a potential exit.

I: Identify Exit Path

Identify your exit path. Are you looking to do an IPO, merge with another company, or find potential buyers for your business? Identifying the possible or desired exit path involves deciding which works best for your business and your goals. This could include selling to individuals, to investors, to competitors, or to other companies within your industry. You can even use various channels such as business brokers, online marketplaces, networking, or direct outreach.

T: Terms and Taxes

Once you have interested buyers, negotiate the terms of the sale. This includes discussing the purchase price, payment structure transition period, noncompete agreements, and other relevant terms. You'll also want to discuss the proposed terms with your Profit Team to make sure you can minimize tax liability and/or set up any beneficial structures in advance prior to constructing the deal.

S: Structure the Deal

Work with your legal and financial advisors to draft a comprehensive agreement that structures and outlines all the terms of the deal and conditions of the sale. This may involve transferring licenses, permits, contracts, and other assets. Depending on the structure of the deal, you may need to assist the new owner during a transition period. This could involve training, introductions to key clients or suppliers, and providing support to ensure a smooth handover. Complete the necessary paperwork to transfer ownership of the business to the buyer.

Post-exit Ramp: Finalize

Once the sale is finalized, you should receive payment as per the agreed-upon terms. Ensure all payments are received in full and according to the agreed schedule. Close out any remaining obligations, such as canceling leases, terminating contracts, and settling outstanding debts. Notify employees, customers, suppliers, and other stakeholders about the change in ownership.

Remember, when you decide to sell your business, you're stepping into a complex world of negotiations, paperwork, and uncertainties. If only finding the right buyer was as easy as putting up a "For Sale" sign.

It takes time to connect with potential buyers, pitch your business, and gauge interest. Before we even get to that part, there is a valuation process. This will give you an understanding of what your business could sell for. This is also the time when you will want to discuss structure and exit strategy to minimize taxes and maximize profits, which I also cover later in this chapter.

Once you go through the process of finding a buyer, going through negotiations, and agreeing to terms, then comes the stage of due diligence. Buyers will want to dig deep into your business's finances, operations, and legal standing. Providing all the necessary documents and addressing their concerns can be a lengthy ordeal.

Coupled with legal and regulatory requirements, this can add another layer of complexity. Transferring licenses, permits, and contracts takes time, not to mention navigating tax implications and compliance issues.

Emotionally it can be difficult as well. You've poured your heart and soul into building this business. Letting go can be hard, causing delays as you wrestle with the decision. As entrepreneurs, we often wrap our whole identity into our businesses, so it's important to have patience and resilience in the process, but also to give yourself some grace.

Exit Principle #3: Your Exit Will Be Determined by Numbers, Data, and Metrics

As much as I would love for your business valuation to be determined by your hard work, endless effort, and the blood, sweat, and tears you put into the business, sadly it isn't.

Your valuation, and ultimately the amount of money you may receive for a capital exit, falls back to more tangible factors like numbers, data, and metrics.

Your overall business valuation will consider factors such as the people on your team, the intellectual and proprietary assets you own, the efficiency of your systems and processes, and the profits and consistent cash flow your business generates. This is because each of these elements contributes significantly to the overall current value and potential future value of your business.

Let's break down four key areas that factor into the return you may receive on your valuation: **Profit, People, Processes, and Proprietary.**

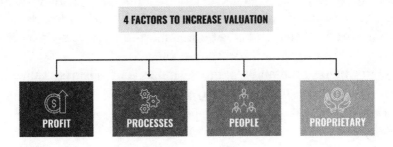

Profit

We have discussed profit in depth throughout this book, and for good reason. Not only is it the foundation that keeps you *in* business, but it's the foundation of what gets you paid when you want to get *out* of business.

The fundamental indicator of your business value and sustainability is profitability.

Unless you're selling individual assets to a potential buyer, and they only see value in pieces of your business and not your business as a whole, potential buyers will want to analyze your financials. They want to see actual revenue, profit margins, cash flow, financial ratios, growth projections, and trajectory, to name a few. They'll want to assess the business's earning potential and return on investment.

Profitability reflects the effectiveness of your business model, market positioning, and operational efficiency. Businesses that have consistent profits and are on a clear growth trajectory are typically valued higher because they offer greater predictability, stability, and potential for generating better returns for the buyer.

Buyers often scrutinize a target company's financial performance, identifying metric rates like profitability, solvency, and operational efficiency. Financial metrics such as gross profit margin, net profit margin, and return on investment offer insights into the company's fiscal health and performance trajectory.

Just like we discussed developing the habit of consistently measuring a few key financial ratios in Chapter 7, these same metrics present themselves here, too. Potential buyers will want to evaluate your liquidity, solvency, and other ratios important to them. Identifying the business's cash flow measures the ability of a business to pay its bills, meet payroll, and cover other short-term expenses as well as have the ability to cover its debts and obligations.

Prioritizing profitability can maximize your business value and your attractiveness to potential buyers.

People

The strength of the people within your business is paramount. Buyers often look for competent and experienced leadership capable of driving growth, managing risks, and executing strategic initiatives effectively.

The skills, expertise, and dedication of your team are invaluable assets to your business. A competent and motivated workforce can drive innovation, enhance productivity, and foster strong customer relationships.

Potential buyers may assess the quality of your employees, including key personnel and management, as they represent the operational backbone and future growth potential of the business. A skilled team often translates into smoother transitions and continued success post-acquisition, enhancing the business's attractiveness and valuation.

A competent and experienced management team is also highly valued by buyers. They may look to evaluate the skills and capabilities of the existing management team and determine whether they have the capacity to drive future growth and manage the business effectively.

The role of people can also extend to the customer base of the business. The long-term satisfaction, loyalty, and retention of a company's customer base are also key considerations of business value. Buyers can assess factors such as customer demographics, retention rates, churn rate, and recurring revenue streams to gauge the stability and growth potential of the business.

Processes

While it seems that very few entrepreneurs are excited to jump out of bed and create processes and systems in their business, having them is mission critical – not just in an exit scenario, but also while you're still in growth and scale.

Experienced founders, and those experienced in acquisitions, know that efficient and well-defined operational processes are essential for maximizing productivity, minimizing costs, and ensuring consistent product/service quality. Having streamlined processes will enhance scalability, improve agility, and overall optimize business performance. Potential buyers will want to assess the effectiveness of your processes and systems to evaluate any operational risks, growth opportunities, and integration challenges.

Businesses with optimized processes are more attractive to buyers because they offer efficiency, scalability, and potential for future growth without adding significant restructuring or investment to streamline operations.

This process doesn't have to be complicated. If you were a pastry chef who owned a bakery, you'd have to create recipes for your cakes and cupcakes in order to have someone else bake them.

Processes in your business are just the recipes of how you and the team do things so it's easier to duplicate yourself and your efforts.

When entrepreneurs tell me that they can never leave their business, or that their team is always coming to them with questions, or that they are having the same recurring problems in the business, that's typically due to lack of processes.

Regardless of whether you're preparing your business to sell or you're still in your build, by focusing on streamlining operations, improving efficiency, and implementing robust management systems and processes, you can drive greater profitability and scalability.

Proprietary

Intellectual property (IP) such as patents, trademarks, copyrights, and trade secrets play a pivotal role in protecting your unique innovations, products, and brand identity and they can drive up your overall valuation.

These assets can provide competitive advantages, market differentiation, and barriers to entry for competitors. Potential buyers may evaluate your IP portfolio to gauge its strength, relevance, and potential for future revenue generation. Businesses with robust proprietary assets often command higher valuations and a subsequent return on EBITDA due to the potential for sustained competitive advantage and additional revenue streams.

This can also lean into tangible assets. Buyers will look for owned assets such as equipment, real estate, and inventory. Premium or keyword-rich domain names may have intrinsic value and contribute to the overall valuation of a business, particularly in e-commerce or digital marketing sectors. Customer databases, mailing lists, and subscriber bases represent valuable assets for businesses, especially in subscription-based or recurring revenue models. And access to a loyal customer base and customer insights can drive revenue growth, market expansion, and customer lifetime value, further influencing business valuation.

Other assets like exclusive contracts, licensing agreements, distribution agreements, or partnerships can represent value because these may provide access to unique markets, distribution channels, or proprietary technologies, enhancing the business's competitive position and valuation.

> # The more valuable *you* are to the business, the less valuable the *business* is to buy.

In addition, any investments in research and development (R&D) activities, proprietary technologies, or innovative solutions can be considered in an evaluation. Intellectual property can commonly be overlooked; however, it can be massively valuable and potentially increase your overall business value as well as the multiple you may receive.

The Role of Valuation

Valuation, in exiting a business, refers to the process of determining the monetary worth of the business. It's crucial because it sets the stage for negotiations between the seller and potential buyers and is critical in the sale or transfer of ownership of the business.

It helps sellers determine the asking price for their business and provides a baseline for negotiations while helping buyers assess risks, make informed decisions, and determine a fair offer price. There are several methods to determine valuation. Here are three:

- **Income approach:** This method looks at the present value of future income streams generated by the business, often using techniques like cash flow analysis.
- **Market approach:** This compares the business to similar companies that have been sold recently, using multiples like price-to-earnings ratios.
- **Asset approach:** This method values the business based on its assets minus liabilities, including tangible and intangible assets.

Some valuation approaches combine elements of the income, market, and asset-based approaches to provide a comprehensive assessment of the business's value and can be tailored to the specific characteristics of the business and industry.

In the sections above, we already discussed several factors that will be considered when figuring out how much a business is worth, but let's dive in a little deeper.

The role of valuation is to determine how well the business is doing financially and evaluating the factors discussed above, including how much revenue it's generating, what is the current growth trajectory, and how much profit is translating to the bottom-line.

Next, they'll take a look at the market the business is in. Is it a growing industry? How well does the business stack up against its competitors? Businesses in hot, growing sectors can achieve higher valuations because they have more potential for making money in the future.

They'll also consider what the business owns and owes. This places value on the business's tangible assets (like buildings, equipment, technology, patents, trade secrets) and subtracts any debts it has while adding value on the intangible assets (customer relationships, brand equity, market positioning, content and media assets, employee loyalty and expertise). The more the business owns and the less it owes can create an overall higher valuation.

A patent for a new invention, a really well-known brand name, or a loyal customer base can make the business more valuable. And as I shared, the people in the business also matter to the valuation. Having a strong management team, layered organizational chart, and an efficiently run operation (without heavily relying on the founder) can make a big difference in the business's overall value.

On the flipside, higher risks usually mean a lower valuation. Risks that might affect the business's future include possible changes in the market, new regulations, or tough competition.

Finally, timing. The reason and timing of *when* you sell can be equally as important as *what* you actually sell. Sometimes waiting for the right moment can lead to a higher valuation, while selling in a hurry can lead to a lower valuation.

I see entrepreneurs get the idea to sell when they lose steam or are hit with one of the five Ds. In those times, if you can find it in you to hang on, then do it, because during exhaustion or a tragedy is never the best time to sell.

When you go to make your capital exit, you want to come from as much of a position of strength and patience as you can because the most ideal time to sell is when your business is in its prime.

There are five common reasons a company dissolves, closes its doors, or is sold at a fraction of its worth. These are the *least favorable* times to sell a business and they are often referred to as **the five Ds of business exits**:

- Death
- Divorce
- Disability
- Disagreement
- Distress

Exiting can be an emotional experience for many entrepreneurs. But just imagine trying to navigate the complexities of that important transaction while dealing with one of the five Ds. To exit the business on your terms, for the highest valuation, you need to start thinking about your plan today.

Exit Principle #4: Your Exit Will Look Different Than You Think

Even with the best-laid plans, your exit will likely look different than expected because, well, most of them do.

It's no secret that real estate or stock markets can take an unexpected turn without notice; the same can be true with mergers and acquisitions. Potential buyers, or the acquiring company, can completely change directions or lose interest. There can be valuation disagreements, legal or compliance hoops to jump through, not to mention that negotiation dynamics play a significant role, impacting the final terms and timing of the exit.

In addition to numbers and the valuation in an exit, there is a real human side of things – emotions, relationships, and personal factors can all make the process difficult to navigate. Essentially, a business exit can feel like sailing through a sea of choppy waters – you need to stay flexible, keep an eye on the horizon, and be ready to adjust and course correct when necessary to reach your destination.

Although it may seem counterintuitive, creating an exit strategy may actually be one of the most important components of your business plan. Any major business decision requires careful strategy and planning. Exiting your business is no exception.

Imagine if you only started planning for a major project or a new product rollout just a few days before its launch date; that would likely end in disaster and be a huge mistake. In the same light, waiting to plan your business exit when you're burned out, uninspired, or ready to retire could lead to missed opportunities, low returns, and costly errors.

Just as with any other business initiative, early and thorough planning is essential. Sadly, far too many smart, capable, and hardworking founders find themselves scrambling when they want to sell their business. The root cause is typically straightforward: they failed to establish an exit strategy well in advance.

A study from the Exit Planning Institute found that more than 64% of founders don't have an exit strategy. What's also shocking is that over half of all current businesses in the United States are owned by the Baby Boomers. Those founders are all set to transition out of entrepreneurship and into retirement in the next one to 10 years – and approximately 80% of those entrepreneurs won't get paid to exit their businesses.[1]

The journey of building a scalable, sustainable, and sellable business can take years, even decades, sometimes stretching over a significant portion of the founder's life – don't you want to get paid for that journey?

Look, if you are reading this and you are years, or decades, into your business realizing you haven't planned for an exit, don't panic. It's common for founders to be so busy building their business, growing their teams, acquiring customers, and navigating through the complexities of entrepreneurship that it's no surprise that crafting an exit strategy didn't top the list of urgent and important tasks. The good news is that there are steps you can take now to prepare yourself, and your business, for a successful exit.

Exit planning is a comprehensive strategy to optimize value, minimize taxes, and ensure a smooth transition for all stakeholders. By starting your plan early, you can be proactive on addressing potential obstacles, building value, and position the business for a successful exit when the time is right.

Here are four things **Entrepreneurs Should Be Doing *Now*** to start creating your exit plan:

1. **Create your vision:** Define your long-term objectives and vision for your exit. Determine what you hope to achieve financially, professionally, and personally through the exit process. Having clear goals will guide your planning and decision-making. Remember that you don't have to say goodbye to your company just because you are selling it. Many exit strategies can involve you still being a part of the company, whether as an advisor, consultant, or board member. (I covered much of this in Chapter 10.)

2. **Conduct a financial valuation:** You may think that your exit is a lifetime down the road, and you may be right. However, assessing the current value of your business and identifying areas for improvement to maximize its value can be beneficial now. By working with financial experts to conduct a thorough valuation and financial analysis of your business – considering factors such as revenue, profitability, assets, liabilities, and market trends – you can gain an understanding of the current value of the business. This process can also give you clarity on what to change in the business to improve your finances and increase the overall valuation.

3. **Identify potential buyers:** Identifying potential buyers for your business requires understanding your industry, market, and ultimately your goals. Start by asking this simple question: Who could potentially be a great buyer for this business? You can start by exploring investors, strategic partnerships, or successors, as well as companies or individuals who may be interested in acquiring a business similar to yours. If you're looking at potentially being acquired by another business, you can look at companies in complementary or related industries, as well as private equity firms or venture capitalists with a track record of acquiring businesses in your sector. You can also consider working with a business broker, investment banker, or M&A advisors who specialize in facilitating business acquisitions and have access to potential buyers.

4. **Create a timeline:** Develop a timeline for your exit plan, including any specific milestones and key deadlines you may have. This enables you to anticipate potential obstacles or challenges

as well as develop contingency plans to address them effectively. Remember, timelines and deadlines are great, but flexibility and adaptability are also crucial for writing and executing your exit strategy. Having an idea on a timeline, but being open to all possibilities, puts you in a stronger position, which can result in a better outcome.

All founders will exit their business at some point. The question is whether it will be on your terms, your timeline, and if you will be paid to do so. You may have a picture in your mind of what an ideal exit looks like, but there are many different exit strategies. Let's get into those now.

The Different Routes to Your Exit

Just as there are a variety of ways to start a business, there are a variety of ways to sell one, too.

It starts by exploring the various strategies because there are numerous paths you can take, each with its own set of considerations and implications. It's important to evaluate the benefits and challenges with each option.

Factors like your business's industry, size, financial health, growth trajectory, and your overall goals will all influence which path is the most suitable for you. By understanding the distinct characteristics of each exit strategy, you can make informed decisions that pave the way for a successful transition and one that secures your legacy.

Let's break down seven common exit strategies for businesses and explore the benefits and challenges of each:

1. **Selling to a New Owner:** This type of exit involves selling your business to an outside party who is not involved in your business or within your family.

   Benefits: Selling your business can provide you with a lump sum of cash, allowing you to potentially secure your financial future.

   Challenges: It can be complex and time consuming to find the right buyer. Ensuring a smooth handover requires careful planning, communication, and coordination between the seller and the new owner. Any disruptions during the transition period can impact the business's operations, employees, clients, and overall performance.

2. **Selling to Another Business:** Mergers and acquisitions (M&A) transactions occur when an existing business is purchased by, or merged with, another existing business. Larger companies may acquire smaller ones for various reasons, such as eliminating competitors or expanding into new markets. Selling your business to another business is often referred to as acquisition. However, in a merger, two companies combine their operations into a single entity.

   Existing owners may retain a management or leadership role in a merger, whereas in acquisitions, founders typically relinquish control to the acquiring company. This can be a complex yet rewarding process.

   Benefits: M&As can result in highly profitable exits, especially in competitive bidding scenarios. Strategic mergers or acquisitions can provide access to greater resources – capital, technology, distribution channels, or talent – leading to new growth opportunities by combining strengths and market positions. This can have massive value creation for both parties because it also can mitigate risks associated with market volatility or economic downturns.

   Challenges: Selling your business to another business can be more complex when it comes to financing, due diligence, and legal complexities as well as integration of the teams, and reassuring and retaining customers throughout the transition. M&A can be time consuming, costly, and may not always succeed, while lengthy noncompete agreements may restrict future business endeavors.

   But the risk can be worth the reward. Successfully managing a merger or acquisition will boil down to strategic planning, effective communication, and a commitment to the long-term vision of both the acquiring and acquired businesses.

3. **Selling to a Known Buyer:** This type of exit involves selling the business to a familiar buyer, such as a partner, investor, family member, or friend.

Benefits: A known buyer can minimize disruption and secure employees and customers in the transition, as well as ensure continued business success.

Challenges: Sellers may feel limited in negotiating terms, potentially resulting in a below-market price, and personal relationships may be strained by a business transaction.

4. **Initial Public Offering (IPO):** An IPO involves a private business becoming public by selling shares in the company. This transition means the business shifts from being primarily backed privately by investors and founders to being partially owned by public shareholders. After an IPO, founders and initial investors may choose to sell their shares or remain involved in the company. Even if they decide to sell, founders and management typically stay on board for a transition period.

   Benefits: An IPO can raise significant capital, facilitating business growth that can give founders and investors the option to cash in on their shares.

   Challenges: IPO exits can be slow, costly, and complex to negotiate. High regulatory costs and extensive reporting requirements are typically required and the stock performance may disappoint founders and investors. The increased timeline brings increased scrutiny and pressure from shareholders and regulatory bodies.

5. **Private Equity Firm:** A private equity (PE) firm raises capital to acquire ownership stakes or buyouts in companies. They often make strategic investments in the business to drive growth and profitability, or to optimize and enhance the performance of the business before ultimately selling or exiting to generate greater returns.

   Benefits: PE firms have substantial financial resources that can fuel growth and expansion while bringing expertise, experience, and a network to help the business accelerate. They can provide strategic guidance and support to create more value in the business, thus creating a more significant payout.

Challenges: PE firms typically have a finite investment horizon and may prioritize short-term profitability over long-term initiatives. The timing and method of the exit are largely dependent on market conditions and may not align with the business owner's preferences or expectations.

6. **Management and Employee Buyouts (MBO):** MBOs involve selling the business to its current management team or employees.

   Benefits: MBOs are typically faster to execute compared to other exit strategies, while business continuity and employee retention are usually high. MBOs can involve fewer parties and less complex negotiations compared to other exit strategies, potentially leading to a faster transaction, and can also offer tax advantages for both sides.

   Challenges: Success depends on sufficient interest and funds within the management team or employees. If the company's financials are weak or unfavorable, financing can be difficult to secure. The process can also be time-consuming and resource-intensive, potentially diverting attention away from day-to-day operations, which could impact business performance.

7. **Liquidation:** In cases of business failure or poor performance, liquidation involves selling off assets to settle debts and/or repay shareholders. It provides the lowest financial returns of the seven exit strategies.

   Benefits: Liquidation can be a quick method to end a business. It provides finality to the venture and can prevent bankruptcy.

   Challenges: Liquidation typically results in a low return on the exit and the business closure negatively impacts employees, partners, and customers, as well as potentially the founders and investors.

Understanding these exit strategies and their respective benefits and challenges can help you make informed decisions about the future and which path might align best for your business.

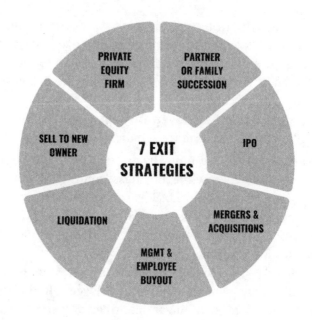

The Holy Grail of Exit: EBITDA

For entrepreneurs eyeing capital exits from their businesses, taking steps to enhance value and prepare for acquisition is key. In the world of business acquisitions, understanding the nuances of how your business will be valued can make all the difference in your eventual payout.

Earlier in the chapter we talked about profit, people, processes, and proprietary as four key factors that can increase your valuation. These components make up a broader framework of your business's valuation. To pursue this further, and dive deeper into the first factor, profit, our focus narrows in and turns to EBITDA.

EBITDA – earnings before interest, taxes, depreciation, and amortization – has been the holy grail of exit because it provides a clear picture of a company's performance. This key metric is used by buyers, sellers, investors, and financial analysts for assessing a company's value, particularly in exit scenarios.

It also simplifies the valuation process by offering a standardized and trusted measure of a company's earnings, making it easier for buyers to compare different businesses and assess their investment potential. This is a preferred metric in many acquisition transactions and is crucial for buyers when evaluating a business's financial health and sustainability.

By focusing on EBITDA you can enhance your business attractiveness for a potential future exit. Even if an exit is a way off, or not a part of your overall plan at all, focusing on these strategies can be the levers that take your business to the next level, now. Here are six strategies that you can proactively implement to increase EBITDA:

1. **Increase your revenue:** Consider focusing on growing your top-line revenue by expanding your customer base, introducing new products or services, or entering new markets, because an increase in revenue can potentially offer more value and a greater return.

2. **Optimize for profit:** Streamline operations, reduce costs, and improve efficiency across all functions of your business to maximize profitability. You can renegotiate supplier contracts, tighten inventory management, or leverage technology to automate processes. Prioritizing profitability and sustainability can enhance overall financial performance, making it more attractive.

3. **Strengthen your customers:** By focusing on customer relationships and systemized acquisition, you can increase retention rates and lifetime value. By implementing customer loyalty programs, investing in customer retention, and soliciting feedback to improve customer satisfaction, you can build a loyal customer base and sustainable revenue streams that any potential buyer would envy.

4. **Diversify your offers:** Buyers want stability in a transaction and to mitigate as much risk as possible. By reducing any dependency on a single product, service, or even a customer segment, you can create a more balanced approach by diversifying revenue streams, minimizing risk, and increasing stability.

5. **Make strategic investments:** This can include investing in research and development, technology, marketing initiatives to drive growth, employee training and development, or by recruiting and retaining top talent for your management team. Making strategic investments that have the potential to generate long-term value and drive growth can result in maximizing EBITDA.

6. **Manage your debt:** Conduct a thorough evaluation of your debt obligations. Review interest rates, repayment terms, and overall debt to find opportunities to refinance at lower interest rates, extend repayment options, or secure more flexibility in terms. Reducing debt through restructuring or even asset sales can improve EBITDA and can enhance the financial stability and resilience of your business.

And regardless of whether you're looking to exit your business in the next couple of years or in the next 20 years, always maintain accurate and up-to-date financial records. This doesn't just serve you in an exit later. It will also help you with growth or scale now.

By building your businesses with the end in mind and focusing on factors that enhance EBITDA and overall profitability, you can position your business for successful exit and maximize value for you and your family. Like business, the landscape of acquisitions continually evolves. Understanding the significance of metrics like EBITDA and other key aspects buyers evaluate is essential for both buyers and entrepreneurs to be successful with their goals.

Exit Principle #5: Your Exit Will Likely Feel Different Than You Imagine

Personally, I was shocked to experience the mixed emotions of letting go of a business. Throughout one exit, I felt pure joy and relief, while the second was excitement and exhaustion mixed with the feeling of "Is this the right decision?"

I've worked with founders who were headed to the signing table with a mix of anxiety or reluctance, and started to hesitate, delay, or try to make unnecessary changes in the exit plan.

Emotional attachment, personal relationships, and a variety of psychological factors can influence decision-making and behavior during the exit process.

My client Kristen poured her heart and soul into building her business from the ground up. For 13 years, she was dedicated to turning it into a success. Along the way, she built a strong team, forged lasting customer relationships, and became a respected leader in her industry.

As the years passed, Kristen began to feel a sense of restlessness and even a pang of resentment creep in. Despite her business's success, she found herself longing for something more – freedom. While she had poured her time and energy into building her business, she realized she had inadvertently lost her own freedom along the way.

When Kristen reached out to hire me, she initially expressed interest in scaling her business and finding a strategic partner to help take her to the next level. But as we went deeper into her true goals and aspirations, it became clear that what Kristen truly desired was something she didn't realize she wanted, or even thought was possible.

Once she gained that clarity, we embarked on a journey to create an exit plan and source a buyer for her business. It was a rollercoaster of emotions for Kristen – excitement, apprehension, nervousness, overwhelm, and everything in between. There were moments of doubt and uncertainty, wrestling with the idea of letting go of the business she had poured her heart and soul into for over a decade.

But through it all, she remained steadfast in her determination to pursue freedom and the ability to move south to be with her family. And after a little over a year of working together, the perfect buyer came into view, someone who shared Kristen's vision for the future of the business and valued her contributions as its founder. She made the bold decision to cash out of her equity – giving her the ultimate chance to reclaim her freedom and autonomy.

The day Kristen closed the deal and officially exited her business was bittersweet. She was excited, relieved, and overcome with emotion that she could now be with her family. And even with all that happiness and pride, she couldn't help but feel an ache of sadness and loss. After all, this business had been her identity for so many years.

But as she walked away from the signing table, Kristen felt a weight lifted off her shoulders – a sense of freedom she hadn't felt in years. Yes, she had lost a part of herself in selling her business, but she had gained so much more in return – the freedom to pursue new passions, spend time with loved ones, and live life on her own terms.

During our last session together, I reflected on the journey that had brought her to this place. Kristen had an immense sense of love for her business, her clients, and her team. She genuinely enjoyed her work but also knew somewhere deep down that although this business got her to where she was, it wasn't going to get her to where she was being called to go. She learned that sometimes, the path to true happiness and fulfillment isn't always what we expect.

In my experience, I have found that exits are like a microcosm of business, even life in general. While it might not align perfectly with what you want, sometimes it ends up being precisely what you need.

While you're navigating this path, I want you to remember this: your current reality, and everything you think you want next, is all based on the past – your past experiences, your past behaviors, your past decisions, and your past environments. What you can achieve, create, and therefore have is far greater than your mind can even comprehend in this moment.

Once we see how our past conditioning is controlling our thoughts and beliefs, thus keeping us where we are, the question to ask is this: If my success were guaranteed, what would I do?

Whether it's growing a business, exiting a company, ringing the opening bell, starting a nonprofit, or expanding your family – know that success is attainable when you have clarity on what you want, and understand what's truly possible.

More Profit, More Impact

Although we've reached the end of this book together, in many ways it's just the beginning. Before we conclude our time together, and as you start the path to building more revenue, more profit, and more freedom, I want to acknowledge *you*.

Being an entrepreneur my entire life, I know how lonely this road can be. I know how at times you feel like you know exactly what you're doing, and how at times you can feel completely lost – and sometimes how those two things can happen within five minutes of each other.

I am constantly inspired by those of you who are dreaming big dreams, accomplishing big things, taking big risks, and making a big impact in the world. And by picking up this book, and reading through to the end, I know that's you.

As you start to apply the principles in *The 9% Edge*, I want to leave you with one final thought. The world will promise you happiness and tempt your ego with flashes and images of what your success in business should look like. But I want to throw a flag of caution.

You can build more revenue, generate more profit, and create more freedom, but doing so without contributing to something beyond yourself, without giving generously, will not give you what you think you're after. Because the key to fulfillment and richness of life isn't found in the accumulation of more; it's found in the contribution of what you do with it.

Perhaps your quest for more revenue, more profit, and more freedom won't just serve your business, but will serve other areas of your life all together. Maybe the pursuit for more enables you to donate to a nonprofit, bless your church, or give to your community – giving *you* the ability to do more, give more, and impact more with what you have.

While you are on your path to becoming part of the 9% who builds a successful, sustainable business, don't forget to build what matters most. Creating a company may give you success by society's standards, but creating a rich life filled with deep meaning, impact, and contribution – *that* is where true fulfillment lies. Joining the 9% will come from *what* you do, but the **Edge** is found in *why* you do it.

Notes

Chapter 1

1. Perry, M.J. 2014. Fortune 500 firms in 1955 vs. 2014; 88% are gone, and we're all better off because of that dynamic "creative destruction." American Enterprise Institute, August 18, https://www.aei.org/carpe-diem/fortune-500-firms-in-1955-vs-2014-89-are-gone-and-were-all-better-off-because-of-that-dynamic-creative-destruction/.
2. Denning, S. 2013. Peggy Noonan on Steve Jobs and Why Big Companies Die. Forbes, June 30, https://www.forbes.com/sites/stevedenning/2011/11/19/peggy-noonan-on-steve-jobs-and-why-big-companies-die/?sh=2321721dcc3a.
3. Rivis, C. 2023. The Predicted Fate of Fortune 500 Companies: A Visionary Perspective. LinkedIn, July 22, https://www.linkedin.com/pulse/predicted-fate-fortune-500-companies-visionary-carlo-rivis/.
4. Oxford English Dictionary. 2023. s.v. "intentionality (n.)," https://doi.org/10.1093/OED/5711438369.
5. Kuvshinikov, P.J., and Kuvshinikov, J.T. 2023. Forecasting Entrepreneurial Motivations and Actions: Development and Validation of the Entrepreneurial Trigger Scale. *Journal of Small Business and Enterprise Development* 31 (8): 1–21. https://doi.org/10.1108/jsbed-06-2022-0274.

Chapter 2

1. Jachimowicz, J.M. 2019. 3 Reasons It's so Hard to "Follow Your Passion." *Harvard Business Review,* October 15, https://hbr.org/2019/10/3-reasons-its-so-hard-to-follow-your-passion.
2. Chen, G., Kim, K., Nofsinger, J.R., and Rui, O.M. 2007. Trading Performance, Disposition Effect, Overconfidence, Representativeness Bias, and Experience of Emerging Market Investors. *Journal of Behavioral Decision Making* 20 (4): 425–451. https://doi.org/10.1002/bdm.561.

Chapter 3

1. SiliconANGLE. 2023. Amazon Delivers Surprisingly Good Earnings Results as AWS Growth Starts to Stabilize, August 4, https://siliconangle.com/2023/08/03/amazon-delivers-surprisingly-good-earnings-results-aws-growth-starts-stabilize.

Chapter 4

1. Stice, J. 2015. McDonald's Most Profitable Items: Running a Profitable Business: Understanding Financial Ratios, https://www.linkedin.com/learning/running-a-profitable-business-understanding-financial-ratios/mcdonald-s-most-profitable-items; Quora. n.d. How Much Does It Cost McDonald's to Make a Hamburger or Cheeseburger and How Much Profit Does McDonald's Make per Burger Sold? https://www.quora.com/How-much-does-it-cost-McDonalds-to-make-a-hamburger-or-cheeseburger-and-how-much-profit-does-McDonalds-make-per-burger-sold.

Chapter 5

1. S&P Global Market Intelligence. n.d. Industries Most and Least Impacted by COVID-19 from a Probability of Default Perspective - January 2022 Update. https://www.spglobal.com/marketintelligence/en/news-insights/blog/industries-most-and-least-impacted-by-covid-19-from-a-probability-of-default-perspective-january-2022-update.
2. Google for Developers. n.d. You and site performance, sitting in a tree. . . Google Search Central Blog, https://developers.google.com/search/blog/2010/05/you-and-site-performance-sitting-in.
3. Fischer, A., and Zuckerman, A. 2022. The Impact of Review Volume on Conversion: Is More Really Better? PowerReviews, March 9, https://www.powerreviews.com/blog/review-volume-conversion-impact/?ref=momentcrm.com.
4. Ibid.
5. Ibid.

Chapter 9

1. BET. 2023. Magic Johnson Is a Billionaire: 5 Things to Know About His Business Ventures. BET, October 31, https://www.bet.com/article/na61qy/magic-johnson-is-a-billionaire-5-things-to-know-about-his-business-ventures; Elkins, K. 2018. How Magic Johnson Convinced Howard Schultz to Partner with Him and Build More Starbucks Stores. CNBC, November 10, https://www.cnbc.com/2018/11/09/how-magic-johnson-got-starbucks-ceo-howard-schultz-to-partner-with-him.html.

2. Yaqub M. 2023. 11 Small Business Accounting Statistics 2023: The Facts and Trends, August 18, https://www.businessdit.com/small-business-accounting-statistics/.

Chapter 10

1. Exit Planning Institute. n.d. The State of Owner Readiness, https://exit-planning-institute.org/state-of-owner-readiness.
2. Sostrin, J. 2021. To Be a Great Leader, You Have to Learn How to Delegate Well. *Harvard Business Review,* April 1, https://hbr.org/2017/10/to-be-a-great-leader-you-have-to-learn-how-to-delegate-well.
3. Business Insights Blog. 2020. How to Delegate Effectively: 9 Tips for Managers. Harvard Business School Online, January 14, https://online.hbs.edu/blog/post/how-to-delegate-effectively.
4. TAMUCC. 2022. What Is the Difference Between a Leader and a Manager? September 14, https://online.tamucc.edu/degrees/business/mba/general/difference-between-leader-and-manager/.
5. MindTools Content Team. n.d. Henri Fayol's principles of management. Mind Tools, https://www.mindtools.com/asjiu77/henri-fayols-principles-of-management.
6. Botelho, E.L. 2017. 4 Things That Set Successful CEOs Apart. *Harvard Business Review,* July 18, https://hbr.org/2017/05/what-sets-successful-ceos-apart.
7. Duffy, C. 2021. Jeff Bezos is stepping down as Amazon CEO. He'll still have huge power at the company. CNN, 5 July, https://www.cnn.com/2021/07/05/tech/jeff-bezos-amazon-ceo-exit/index.html.
8. Hayes, A. 2023. Where Does Bill Gates Keep His Money? Investopedia, April 17, https://www.investopedia.com/articles/personal-finance/111214/where-does-bill-gates-keep-his-money.asp.

Chapter 11

1. Exit Planning Institute. n.d. The State of Owner Readiness, https://exit-planning-institute.org/state-of-owner-readiness.

Acknowledgments

As I reflect back on the pages of this book, I'm filled with immense gratitude to so many people who helped along my journey.

Starting my first business feels like a lifetime ago. To that 19-year-old girl I once was—thank you for taking the risks, for going after it all, and for fighting so hard for us to get here.

However, first and foremost, God gets the glory. I have doubted myself and my abilities throughout the different chapters of my life, but I find strength when I remember that "God doesn't call the qualified, He qualifies the called" (1 Corinthians 1:27).

Secondly, I want to thank all of those who made this book possible. Without your work, research, and support, this book wouldn't be here. Thank you to the incredible team at Wiley for bringing this book to life. A huge thank-you to Julie Kerr for her work editing and helping me communicate my work more clearly. Jasmine Jonte, thank you for supporting the visual concepts within this book, and Daniel Decker for being my first domino.

To the authors and founders before me who shared their wisdom with the world, thank you for giving me a real-world education in business. And to Tony Robbins, I'll be forever grateful; you've been such an inspiration in my life.

Thank you to my clients – the dreamers, the doers, the risk-takers, the implementers, and those courageous enough to be relentless in the pursuit of growth – you inspire me every day.

To Jerry Answine, it was such a joy to work with you for all of those years. I hope you're up there scoring eagles on every hole.

Thank you to my family for putting up with me writing and rewriting on every holiday, vacation, and trip. To my friends—thank you for your patience and grace as I basically disappeared for over a year. To my friend Anne Degre, who passed far too soon—thank you for your example of strength and resilience. Thank you to Grace, who never left my side as I wrote through the late nights and early mornings.

And this would not be complete without thanking you, the reader. Thank you for supporting my work and this book – words cannot begin to express my gratitude.

Last, but certainly not least, Anthony. Thank you for your encouragement, belief, and support throughout this crazy life, as well as patiently waiting for me to finish this book to finally get married.

About the Author

Being born into poverty and raised on government assistance meant that Candy Valentino's early life wasn't about privilege but merely survival.

A founder before she could legally order a drink, Candy started her business with no money, no degree, and no corporate background at just 19. She went on to grow, scale, and exit multiple businesses in various industries as well as investing in real estate for more than two and a half decades.

At just 26, she founded a nonprofit and donated a building to the organization. She was actively involved in the mission for over 16 years, personally raising millions and saving thousands of animals' lives while developing programs to help abused animals and underprivileged children.

During her two and a half decades as an entrepreneur, she has been named to Top Business Leaders 40 Under 40, Top 50 Women in Business, 10 People Making a Difference, Top 10 Business Consultants by Yahoo Finance, and was the youngest female to receive the Governor's Award in Entrepreneurship. *Success* magazine named her one of the "Women of Influence," and she has been listed with "Leaders Who Get Results" alongside Tony Robbins and Brené Brown.

Candy is a frequent media guest and highly sought-after speaker on topics like business growth and finance, wealth, and investing. She's been featured in numerous TV, radio, magazine, and newspaper articles including *Forbes, Success,* Yahoo Finance, Oprah Daily, CNBC Make It, and BBC World Report – not only for business and investing but for her advocacy and philanthropic work. She was also named one of Arizona's "Persons of Distinction."

After exiting her last company, Candy started sharing real-world business and investing strategies, gathering an audience of millions.

She is a published author, the CEO of Founders Organization, and host of the podcast *The Candy Valentino Show,* featuring in-depth conversations with some of the most successful minds, including Tony Robbins, Daymond John, Ed Mylett, and Jamie Kern Lima, alongside valuable insights drawn directly from Candy's 26 years of expertise.

Her book *Wealth Habits*: *Six Ordinary Steps to Achieve Extraordinary Financial Freedom,* and her children's book, *Dream Big: Because Anything Is Possible,* hit multiple bestseller lists, including topping the *Wall Street Journal* Bestseller List.

Learn more about programs and events at **www.candyvalentino.com** and find Candy on all social media platforms under @candyvalentino.

Wealth Habits Cover

Wealth Habits QR Code

The Candy Valentino Show Cover

The Candy Valentino Show QR Code

Index